The American Exploration and Travel Series

*British
Travelers
Among the
Southern
Indians, 1660-1763*

British Travelers Among the Southern Indians, 1660-1763

J. Ralph Randolph

UNIVERSITY OF OKLAHOMA PRESS : NORMAN

Library of Congress Cataloging in Publication Data
Randolph, J   Ralph, 1935–
      British travelers among the southern Indians, 1660–1763.
      (The American exploration and travel series, v. 62) Bibliography:
      p.
      1. Indians of North America—Southern states. 2. Indians of North
America—Government relations—To 1789. I. Title. II. Series.
E78.S65R3   970.4'5   72–858
ISBN 0–8061–1019–8

Copyright 1973 by the University of Oklahoma Press, Publishing
Division of the University. Composed and printed at Norman, Oklahoma, U.S.A., by the University of Oklahoma Press. First edition.

British Travelers Among the Southern Indians, 1660–1763 is Volume
62 of *The American Exploration and Travel Series*.

For Lee

Acknowledgments

I am grateful to several persons and institutions for assistance in the preparation of the study. The staffs of the Library of Congress, the University of New Mexico, and the University of Texas at Austin rendered courteous and necessary assistance in securing research material. Cherie Edwards Wyatt contributed to the preparation of the maps, and my secretary, Lillian Dees, typed the manuscript and did much of the indexing.

Professor William M. Dabney, teacher, mentor, and friend, made numerous beneficial comments from the genesis of the study. His kind suggestions and continuing faith can never be repaid.

Special thanks are due Southwest Texas State University and especially President Billy Mac Jones, whose encouragement and support made publication of the manuscript possible.

Lee Sullens Randolph, my beloved wife, not only proofread, but also with understanding permitted my frequent absences from our normal home life. Her patience and love contributed immeasurably to the completion of the study.

San Marcos, Texas   J. RALPH RANDOLPH
August, 1972

Contents

xi

Illustrations

xiii

Old man in winter garment
A conjurer
Indians fishing
Indians dancing
Village of Secoton
Byrd's map, 1738
Title page of Lawson's *New Voyage*, 1709
Naire's map of South Carolina, 1711
Deerskin map, 1724
Moll's map of Carolina, 1729
Tomochichi and Tooanahowi
Oglethorpe presenting Tomochichi to Georgia Trustees
Hunter's map of the Cherokee Nation, 1730
A 1744 map of South Carolina by Herbert and Hunter

Following page 144

Cherokees with Cuming in London
Bowen's map of Georgia, 1748
Creek and Choctaw pictographs
A Chickasaw warrior
Two Choctaw Indians
A Creek war chief
Creek council house
Map of Catawba villages, 1750
Mitchell's map of North America, 1755
Manuscript page from Richardson's *Account*, 1758
Title page of Timberlake's *Memoirs*, 1765
Timberlake's map of Cherokee country, 1765
Cherokees in London
Outacite, Cherokee chief
Austenaco
Cunne Shote

xiv

Maps

*British
Travelers
Among the
Southern
Indians, 1660-1763*

Introduction

W HEN Christopher Columbus
recorded his impressions of the native Americans inhabiting a small
West Indies island, he initiated a long series of accounts by European
travelers of the Indians and their civilization. For nearly four centuries after the first voyage of the Admiral of the Ocean Sea, men of
many European countries and their American-born descendants
journeyed into lands unsettled by the whites and encountered the
exotic red man.[1] The Old World strangers were sometimes welcomed
and sometimes killed, but they were nearly always intrigued with
their hosts.

The English were relatively slow in joining the steady stream
of visitors. Not until nearly one hundred years after the voyages of
Columbus and a half-century after the "Gentleman of Elvas," chroni-
cler of the De Soto expedition, recorded the first detailed European
impressions of the Southeastern Indians did the English attempt
colonization and thereby provide frequent opportunities for English
narratives. With the founding of the first permanent English colony

---

[1] Good introductions to the people of the New World, especially North America,
are Harold E. Driver, *Indians of North America*, Clark Wissler, *American Indians, an
Introduction to the Anthropology of the New World*, and Robert F. Spencer *et. al.*, *Native
Americans*. The first two works use a traditional anthropological approach, i.e., cultural
trait location and classification, while the latter discusses Indian civilization by cultural
areas.

in North America, more Englishmen by design or chance had contact with the natives. As the population grew and the colonies increased, the numbers of travelers among the Indians increased likewise. Because of the lack of time or interest in writing or because the accounts have disappeared, the reactions and observations of the majority of travelers are not available, but the narratives of many of these adventurers are known.[2]

For the Southern colonies alone, the invaluable three-volume work edited by Thomas D. Clark, *Travels in the Old South: A Bibliography*, indicates that a sizable number of "travelers" made at least some comment regarding the Southeastern Indians during the colonial period. The number is somewhat misleading because Clark included as "travelers" several individuals who never crossed the Atlantic and others who never stirred outside the settled areas of the colonies. It should be remembered, however, that the work does not normally include travel narratives found in manuscript or printed as articles. *Travels in the Old South* also does not claim to be a comprehensive compilation of all separately published works.[3]

The value of the writings of travelers has long been recognized by scholars in various fields. For example, historians of early Jamestown heavily depend upon the writings of Captain John Smith, as do anthropologists and ethnohistorians for their understanding of the Indians of the Chesapeake Bay. The works of English colonial travelers such as Robert Beverley, William Byrd II, John Lawson, and Henry Timberlake have also been widely consulted by historians and anthropologists endeavoring to comprehend the American Indians and their relation to the English colonies. Students of American literature have depended upon the more famous accounts of Indians for an insight into the literature of the period and for a better understanding of the authors' view of their world. In 1925, Benjamin H.

---

[2] A useful anthology that relies essentially on colonial travel accounts is Wilcomb E. Washburn, ed., *Indian and the White Man*. Newton D. Mereness also edited several accounts of the Indians written by travelers. *Travels in the American Colonies, 1690–1783.*

[3] I, xvii.

Bissell published *American Indian in English Literature of the Eighteenth Century*, and eight years later Albert Keiser followed with *The Indian in American Literature*. Another frequent use made of such colonial narratives is as an introductory portion in studies of American attitudes toward the Indian during the national period. The best general investigation of the nineteenth-century American attitude toward the Indian is Roy H. Pearce's *The Savages of America: A Study of the Indian and the Idea of Civilization*. Lewis O. Saum[4] and Robert F. Berkhofer, Jr.,[5] have recently published excellent accounts of the fur traders and missionaries among the Indians. Each of these authors concentrates heavily on the national period of American history and uses only the best-known accounts for the colonial era.

For reasons that are not readily apparent, historians interested in English travelers in America have concentrated on the national period, and very few studies have been made of colonial travelers. The small amount of work that has been done for the colonial era is concerned almost entirely with commentary on the settled portions of the colonies and in the wilderness immediately adjacent. Percy G. Adams has recently completed a delightful scholarly study of travelers during the colonial period, but he included accounts by men from several European countries. His primary concern was the effect of the books on the reading public and the plagiarisms and hoaxes included by the ingenious authors.[6]

An extensive study devoted exclusively to Englishmen who voluntarily visited the native Americans apparently has never been undertaken. The dramatic aspect of "civilized" man falling victim to the "wild savages" has appealed to writers, and studies have been made of those unfortunate colonial men and women who became captives of the natives.[7] But no one seems to have studied the British who

[4] *Fur Trader and the Indian.*

[5] *Salvation and the Savage: An Analysis of Protestant Missions and the American Indian Response, 1787–1862.*

[6] *Travelers and Travel Liars, 1660–1800.*

[7] Howard H. Peckham, ed., *Captured by Indians; True Tales of Pioneer Survivors.*

willingly traveled among the Indians. What were the social and economic positions of the white visitors? What amount of formal education and worldly experience influenced their impressions of the red men? What exactly were the recorded reactions and observations of the whites upon contact with the natives? A study directed along these lines should provide insight into the eighteenth-century Englishman and his ethnocentrism.

Such a study poses unusual problems for the student of history. To judge the travelers' impressions, some knowledge of the Indians' culture and society as understood by anthropologists and ethnologists is essential. Closely associated is the attention that must be given to travelers' observations of the effect of European civilization on the natives. Finally, although the study would not be centered on the more formal relations of the English colonies and the home government with the Indians, some attention must be given to Anglo-Indian relations because of the effect not only on the whites' willingness to travel west, but also on the sojourners' impressions.

A cursory study of travel accounts, anthropological literature, and the studies of white-Indian relations during the colonial period revealed the impracticality of attempting to study all of the colonies. Englishmen left too many accounts of varying length and detail to be covered in one work. Furthermore, anthropologists have identified more than 125 Indian groups distinguishable as separate societies in the area from Maine to Georgia and from the Atlantic to the Mississippi River.[8] Many of the Indians had somewhat similar cultures and social systems, but the variation in detail and in some cases major aspects of the civilizations was extensive.

Therefore, definite limits have been placed on this study. The geographical area was limited to the Southern colonies, corresponding generally to the anthropologists' Southeastern cultural area of the North American Indians.[9] The territorial limitation was arbitrary;

[8] The tribes are located on the map provided in Harold E. Driver *et. al., Indian Tribes of North America.*

[9] *Ibid.,* and John R. Swanton, *Indians of the Southeastern United States* (2 vols., Bureau of American Ethnology [hereinafter referred to as BAE] *Bulletin 137*), map 1.

profitable studies could be made of the Middle Atlantic colonies and of the New England area. The period of time under consideration was set at 1660–1763.

Roy H. Pearce has said that late colonial writing on Indians was characterized by comparisons to the noble cultures of ancient Greece and Rome.[10] Preliminary examination of travel materials, however, revealed a surprising lack of comment on "Roman" or "Greek" attributes of the red man.

The year 1660 has certain meaning in the writing of American travel accounts. The lull in colonization which occurred during the Civil War and Commonwealth period of English history ended with the restoration of the monarchy. Not only were several new colonies founded and foreign possessions conquered and Anglicized, but the older colonies turned with new attention to the West.[11] All the activity brought increased numbers of travelers into the Indian country. It has been stated, moreover, that a definite continuity exists in the travel accounts beginning in 1660 and continuing for more than a century.[12] The year 1763 is not only the traditional date for the beginning of strife between the colonies and Great Britain, but in the study of travelers among the Indians has another distinction. The end of the final colonial war with France and the expulsion of that country from the continent of North America caused markedly increased British activity in the West.[13]

Some final remarks concerning the study are necessary. The accounts used were written by *bona fide* travelers among the Southeastern Indians. Those by residents, captives, and members of military expeditions have been excluded. The comparison of impressions and knowledge of a man like James Adair, who lived for years among the

The major differences in the location of the Southern colonies and the Southeastern cultural area is that the cultural area does not extend into the Chesapeake Bay area but does extend slightly west of the Mississippi River near the Gulf of Mexico.

[10] Pearce, *Savages of America*, 42–43 *et passim*.

[11] John B. Brebner, *Explorers of North America, 1492–1806*, 284.

[12] Adams, *Travelers and Travel Liars*, 6.

[13] See Thomas P. Abernethy, *Western Lands and the American Revolution*, and Clarence W. Alvord, *Mississippi Valley in British Politics*.

red men, with the observations of as interested a traveler as John Lawson is hardly a comparison of equals. The impressions of prisoners of the Indians and of persons engaged in military actions tend to be highly colored, on the one hand by the distress of captivity and on the other by the desire to defeat the "savage" opponents. An attempt has also been made to use only writings by persons who are known actually to have traveled among the red men. When there was doubt whether a man wrote from personal experience, the narrative has not been used. Accounts by men such as Jonathan Carver, who seemingly did travel among the Indians but chose to take his comments from others, have also been omitted.[14]

The study, therefore, attempts to determine the impressions of the British who willingly traveled among the Southeastern Indians on peaceful missions between 1660 and 1763. The accounts of nearly fifty British subjects[15] of their sojourns among the native Americans of the South during times of peace have been included. With only a few exceptions the exposure of colonial travelers to the native Americans of the South was transitory. The accounts left by these men tend to emphasize the dramatic and easily observable aspects of the host civilization. It is hoped that the quantity and quality of the information provide some insight into the visitors' personal interest and may indicate indirectly the elements of native culture which fascinated British society in general.

The Indians among whom the travelers journeyed were part of the Southeastern cultural area, which extended from the Ohio River Valley south to the Gulf of Mexico and from the Atlantic Ocean to the Mississippi River with some extension westward near the mouth of the Mississippi. The territory visited by the British colonists was not as large. Between 1660 and 1763 the Spanish controlled Florida, and the French held the Mississippi Valley. Subjects of the British

---

[14] Adams, *Travelers and Travel Liars*, 3, 83–86, 203, and Edward G. Bourne, "The Travels of Jonathan Carver," *American Historical Review*, Vol. XI (Jan., 1906), 287–302.

[15] All the writers were men. No travel account by a woman was located.

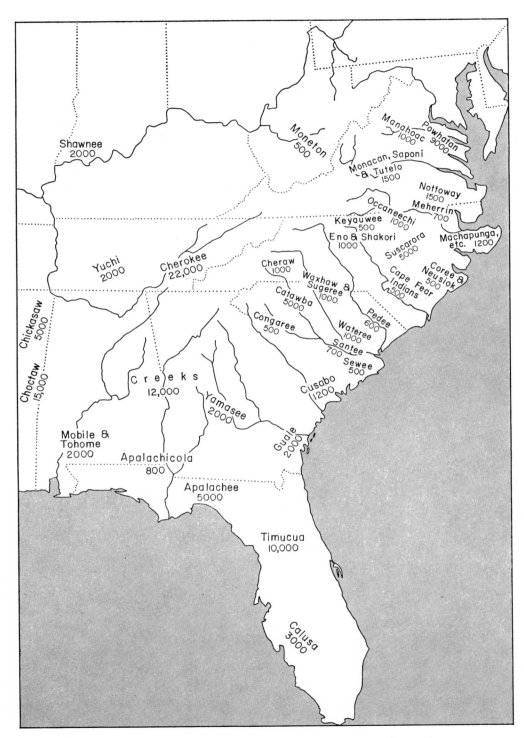

Approximate Population and Location of the Southern Indians, circa 1700

monarchy were not welcome in the domain of the two Roman Catholic powers. Therefore, the British confined their visits to the tribes living between Florida and the Ohio Valley and between the Appalachian Mountains and the Atlantic seaboard.

The westernmost tribes of Indians encountered by the travelers were the Cherokees and members of the Creek Confederation known to whites as the Lower Creeks. The Cherokees were located in the Appalachian Mountains in the region where the present states of North Carolina, South Carolina, Georgia, and Tennessee nearly join. The Lower Creeks inhabited the Piedmont of Georgia. A number of small Siouan tribes were located in the Piedmont-Tidewater region of the Carolinas and Virginia. At the time of European contact, the Siouans had shared the shores of the Chesapeake Bay with Algonkian-speaking groups. But by 1660 the Algonkian tribes had greatly declined in number and importance or had been driven west. North Carolina contained besides some Siouan and Algonkian groups the Tuscaroras and Nottoways who were linguistically affiliated with the Cherokees and the Iroquois of New York. During the second decade of the eighteenth century the Tuscaroras went to war with the English, and following their defeat, they moved north to join the League of the Iroquois.[16]

The land inhabited by the Southern Indians[17] may be divided into three geographical provinces: the Coastal Plain, the Piedmont Plateau, and the Appalachian Mountains. The Coastal Plain extends inland some one hundred to three hundred miles and varies in elevation from sea level to several hundred feet. In the area, generally referred to as the "Tidewater" by the colonists, rivers are sluggish and meander to the ocean. Scrub oak and longleaf and loblolly pine

[16] Indian tribes in the Southeast, as elsewhere, were not stable in location, and the locations given are general. They apply primarily to the period under study. On tribal movements in the area, see Swanton, *Southeastern Indians*, I, 21–33 and map 10. The discussion of the Southern Indians in the remainder of this chapter is based largely upon Swanton's encyclopedic treatment of these Indians. The remarks are intended to summarize the major features of the natives' society and culture.

[17] In the study, the terms Southern and Southeastern Indians are synonymous.

are typical forms of plant life. The transition to the Piedmont Plateau is relatively abrupt and characterized by rapids in the rivers. The Piedmont rises in elevation to about 1,500 feet and is some 150 miles wide at its greatest extent. Forests of pine, oak, gum, and sycamore covered the Piedmont when the English arrived. The Southern Appalachian Mountains rise several hundreds of feet within a few miles to form the Blue Ridge sub-province. West of the Blue Ridge lies the Great Valley which is more than sixty miles wide in Tennessee. The Cumberland Plateau forms the western rim of the Great Valley. North and west of the Appalachians is the Great Interior Plain; to the southwest is found the fertile Black Belt. In the mountains are found hardwood forests, while vegetation in the valleys is similar to that of the Piedmont. Each of the three geographical provinces receives abundant rainfall and the climate is warm. Winters are mild except in the mountainous regions. Most of the area has more than two hundred frost-free days a year.

Edible and useful plants, fruit, roots, nuts, and game are found throughout the Southeast. Indians ate and used in their native crafts a wide variety of the wild life. The most widely cultivated plants were corn, beans, peas, squashes, pumpkins, and tobacco. Cane was a highly useful plant, employed in making baskets, mats, fish traps, sieves, spears, arrows, and torches. It was also used in building houses and fences. Many types of wood were used in the construction of homes, canoes, and mortars. Animals were very important in the livelihood of the Southern Indians, and the deer was the most valuable. The red men ate deer, bear, buffalo, and many smaller animals as well as birds and fish. Some of the tribes also ate snakes, turtles, terrapins, and certain insects. From the hides, furs, and feathers they manufactured their clothing, robes, mantles, and bed coverings. Both sexes anointed their hair and body with bear oil. From bones and sinews came ornaments and string, and horns were boiled to make glue.

The Southeastern Indians lived in two types of houses. One was circular in form and consisted of a framework covered with wattle and mud. Mats were sometimes placed over the mud. The circular building was the typical winter home of the Cherokees and was used as the ceremonial structure of the Creeks and some of the Siouan tribes. The Creeks preferred a rectangular dwelling of similar construction for their homes. Small oval huts, usually called wigwams by the British, were favored by Siouan and Algonkian groups. Many members of all of the Southern tribes moved into arbors and lightly constructed buildings during the warm summer months. Most of the houses had only one door, which faced the east or south, almost always were without windows, and usually had a smoke hole in the roof, although the winter houses often lacked the roof opening. In the latter case, the smoke escaped only through the door. Beds or benches of cane or wooden splints extended around the interior walls of the houses. Mats and animal hides offered the sleeper some comfort and covering. Stockades were used in times of war and were especially useful for outlying villages that were prone to attack.[18]

Details of clothing and ornaments varied with tribes, but there were some general characteristics. Breechclouts for men and skirts reaching to the knees for women were the typical clothes in the Southeast. During cold weather the natives added cloaks and robes to their wardrobes. Moccasins were donned for travel; however, the feet were normally bare. Beads, gorgets, and nose ornaments were widespread. They were usually made of shell, although bone, horn, pearls, and metals were used. Young warriors among the Creeks and Cherokees wove bands of copper, obtained from the Great Lakes region, through slits in their ears. Copper was also used for rings, bracelets, and armbands. Very little gold, silver, or iron was utilized in the area prior to white contact, but after the arrival of Europeans, silver was extensively used for ornaments.

The Indians decorated their bodies in a number of ways. Tattooing was achieved by pricking or cutting the skin and rubbing in soot. Paints were widely employed, especially by the men when pre-

---

[18] *Ibid.,* I, 1–10, 244–48, 386–439; Driver, *Indians of North America,* 28–29, 41–44, 116–18; and David I. Bushnell, Jr., *Native Villages and Village Sites East of the Mississippi* (BAE *Bulletin 69*).

paring for war or ball games. Hair styles varied from tribe to tribe. Many of the Creek and Cherokee warriors shaved the sides of the head, leaving a strip of hair from front to back with a fringe along the forehead. The Siouan tribes usually removed the hair from one side of the head, evidently to prevent entangling the bowstring. All body hair except for that on the head was removed by most of the Indians of both sexes. Women usually wore their hair long, but it might be knotted or rolled. They also commonly cut their hair or permitted it to remain disheveled in times of mourning.[19]

The majority of the Southeastern tribes were composed of matrilineal clans.[20] The clans were of utmost importance in the life of the Indian. Marriage within the clan was strictly forbidden, being considered incest. Punishment for such an offense, as well as for adultery, theft, and murder, was in the hands of the clan members. Clans also played vital roles in the annual ceremonies, the ball games, and the government of the tribe. They were also the landowning units. Many of the tribes also separated the clans into moieties. Each village often had these dual divisions, and occasionally the entire tribe was divided. For example, there were "red" and "white" towns associated respectively with war and peace among the Creeks and Cherokees. There were also "red" and "white" organizations within each town. In times of war the inhabitants of all the towns would engage in the fighting, but the distinctions did have importance. The "red" moiety provided war leaders and war priests while the leaders of the "white" moiety had the most influence in times of peace. Certain ceremonies were traditionally directed by each moiety, and the two groups frequently engaged in the hard-fought ball games which Europeans called lacrosse.[21]

[19] Swanton, *Southeastern Indians*, I, 243, 439–77, 481–508, 510–23, II, 528–36; and John R. Swanton, *Early History of the Creek Indians and Their Neighbors* (BAE *Bulletin 73*), 149, 346.

[20] The Siouans evidently were an exception to the general rule; they probably lacked clans but did have matrilineal descent. See Frank G. Speck, "The Question of Matrilineal Descent in the Southeastern Siouan Area," *American Anthropologist*, n.s., Vol. XL (Jan., 1938), 1–12.

[21] Swanton, *Southeastern Indians*, II, 653–70, 701–709; William H. Gilbert,

The degree of political authority held by native leaders and the means of acquiring the authority varied widely in the Southeast. A mixture of aristocracy and democracy characterized the government of the majority of the tribes. A few individuals exercised uncommon influence because of their ability in hunting or making war or because their counsel was highly regarded. Whatever rank and privileges a man inherited were largely determined by his clan, but in the historic period the rank and importance of the man's father tended to affect his own position. The development probably was a result of white influence. A few individuals such as Powhatan, who ruled many of the Algonkian tribes around the Chesapeake Bay at the beginning of the seventeenth century, did exercise absolute authority, but such power was the exception. Furthermore, Powhatan had created his "empire" by conquest only a short time prior to the arrival of the English.[22]

Although Powhatan enjoyed unusual success in conquering and holding together several Chesapeake Bay tribes, warfare was vital to all the Southern Indians. Because of the relatively small population, the state of native technology, and the vigilance of the defenders, native warfare was probably not excessively destructive, at least until the introduction of European weapons, but scalps and prisoners were highly desired. A male was not considered a man until he had proved himself in war, and no woman desired or was permitted to marry a "boy." The leaders of war parties were elected or at least enjoyed the confidence of the members of the group, and no man was compelled to fight. Even after joining an expedition a man might return home without disgrace if he had a dream or found an omen that caused him to believe that he should not continue. Everyone was welcome to par-

---

"Eastern Cherokees," BAE *Bulletin 133*, 317–18, 321–25, 348–56; and John R. Swanton, "Social Organization and Social Usages of the Indians of the Creek Confederation," BAE *Forty-second Annual Report*, 107–66.

[22] Swanton, *Southeastern Indians*, II, 641–54, 661–62; and Driver, *Indians of North America*, 344–47. In a recent article, William S. Willis argues that the importance of patrilineal institutions in the area has been greatly underestimated in older studies. "Patrilineal Institutions in Southeastern North America," *Ethnohistory*, Vol. X (Summer, 1963), 250–69.

ticipate in the celebrations following the return of a successful war party. If a man had been lost, his female relatives mourned and sought to exact vengeance on any unfortunate prisoner. Prisoners were also occasionally adopted or married into the victorious tribe, and a prisoner might be ransomed.

Warriors preferred a simple costume of paint and a breech-clout but used a large variety of weapons. Bows and arrows, spears and lances, clubs, hatchets, and knives were common and were manufactured in several forms. The natives quickly adopted guns and iron knives and tomahawks when contact was established with Europeans. For defense, shields and perhaps body armor were employed.

The religious beliefs and practices of the Southern Indians were diverse, but most of the red men had some concept of a Superior Being. Cosmogonic myths and legends dealing with man, animals, and supernatural beings were also common. Idols and images of gods evidently were more common among the Algonkian and Siouan tribes than among the Creeks and Cherokees. Equally important, if not more so in the everyday life of individuals, were omens and taboos. Prescribed manners existed for the conduct of warfare, hunting, and, indeed, all significant activities. Dreams and their significance were of great concern, especially among the Cherokees who shared the characteristic with their Iroquois kinsmen. Much of the religious life was expressed through a cycle of ceremonies. One of the most widely distributed ceremonies in the Southeast took place following the corn harvest. The British often referred to it as the "green corn dance," and it was a feast of first fruit. The Indians expressed their thanksgiving for the harvest and their hopes for a continued food supply.[23]

Medicine men were important in the ceremonial life and in the medical practices of the tribes. They usually claimed to have the gift of prophecy, and among some tribes they sought to control the

[23] Swanton, *Southeastern Indians*, II, 564–89, 686–701, 742–82, and "Religious Beliefs and Medical Practices of the Indians of the Creek Confederacy," BAE *Forty-second Annual Report*, 477–636; and James Mooney, "Myths of the Cherokees," BAE *Nineteenth Annual Report*, 239–427.

weather. Healing of the ill was a major concern of the shamans. In the treatments, sympathetic magic, appeals to animal spirits, and expulsion of the influence of witches as well as concoctions of herbs and roots were used. Patients were sometimes scratched or massaged, and the affected area might be sucked or have heat applied to it. The aim of all of these treatments was to remove or drive out the evil spirit. Another common medical practice was the use of sweat houses, but such baths were not usually taken under the direction of shamans. Sweat baths were also widely used for relaxation and to continue good health.

The life of the Southeastern red man ordinarily followed a consistent pattern from one year to the next. Because of climatic and geographical differences there was some variation in the annual cycle, but there was general conformity among most of the tribes. Many of the women, children, and old people remained at home throughout the year; most of the men were absent at least during the annual hunting season. As cold weather approached, or in some cases, well into the winter, the men left to seek game. Some might also join a war party. The length of their absence depended upon the abundance of animals and the men's determination, but normally several months were spent in hunting. In the spring they returned to the village and helped the women plant the crops of corn, beans, and pumpkins. Between planting and harvesting, a shorter hunting expedition was possible. During the harvest time everyone returned and took part in the work and rewards. This was also the period of great celebrations and ceremonies because the people were together and food was abundant. As the nights grew colder the cycle began anew.[24]

The Indian of the Southeastern woodlands was dependent upon the bounties of nature. The forest provided game that fed and clothed him and timber for his home. From the earth came the clays for his pottery and the materials for many of his weapons and ornaments. The European considered native technology to be primitive, but the colonial white seldom attempted to understand the complex

[24] Swanton, *Southeastern Indians*, I, 255–65, II, 742–99.

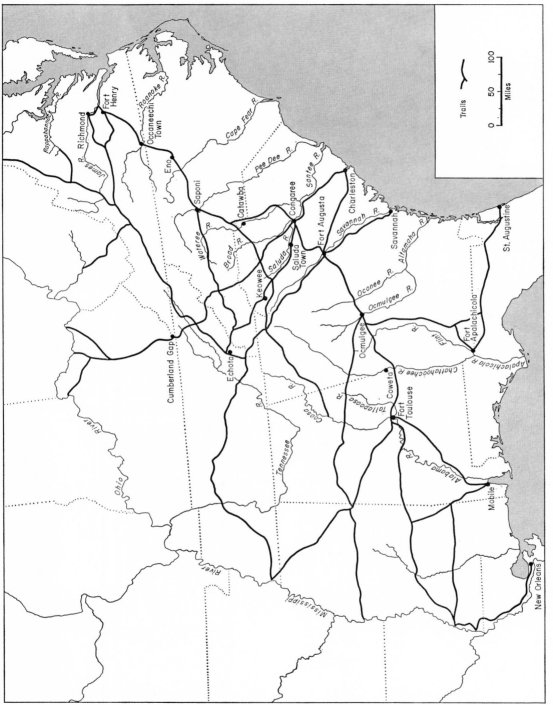

Major Trails in the Southeast, circa 1700

social organization and religious beliefs of the red man. Contacts with the European and his culture caused changes in the civilization of the native. All of the tribes of the Southeast were influenced by white culture during the century following the restoration of the British monarchy. But the explorers of the Virginia Piedmont and the Carolina coast were privileged to observe native life before any meaningful changes had taken place. These adventurers often exhibited little profound interest in the Indian culture, but they did leave valuable accounts of a number of the Southern tribes.

II

Explorers Among the Piedmont and Coastal Indians, 1660–1674

THE period from the restoration of Charles II to the end of the seventeenth century was one of tremendous expansion for the British colonies in North America. In the area north of the Chesapeake Bay, Pennsylvania was founded, and the Dutch possessions were conquered and then permanently occupied. To the south of the Potomac, the Carolinas were settled, and Virginia looked westward toward the Appalachian Mountains. Besides the natural interest that Virginia and the other colonies had in the real and fabled wealth of the West, the explorations of the French spurred the English into activity.[1] As the Englishmen explored the Southern Piedmont and transmontane region or sailed along the Carolina coast seeking suitable sites for European settlements, they usually had some contact with the Indians. The explorers and their sponsors were most interested in the natural resources of the area, and while reports of the expeditions tended to emphasize the quality of the soil and any evidence of mineral riches, encounters with the native Americans were also noted.

In the few years between 1669 and 1674 several major explor-

---

[1] For the importance of the period in the expansion of British North America, see Brebner, *Explorers of North America*, 284, and Clarence W. Alvord and Lee Bidgood, *First Explorations of the Trans-Allegheny Region by the Virginians, 1650–1674*, 56–61, 92–97.

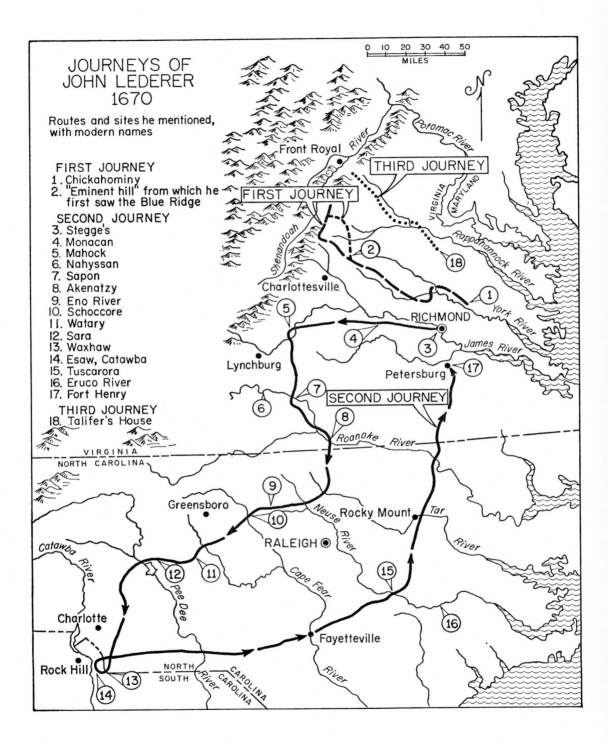

JOURNEYS OF
JOHN LEDERER
1670

Routes and sites he mentioned,
with modern names

FIRST JOURNEY
1. Chickahominy
2. "Eminent hill" from which he
   first saw the Blue Ridge
SECOND JOURNEY
3. Stegge's
4. Monacan
5. Mahock
6. Nahyssan
7. Sapon
8. Akenatzy
9. Eno River
10. Schoccore
11. Watary
12. Sara
13. Waxhaw
14. Esaw, Catawba
15. Tuscarora
16. Eruco River
17. Fort Henry
THIRD JOURNEY
18. Talifer's House

ations were made from Virginia to the West. In 1669 and 1670 John Lederer made three trips into the Piedmont of Virginia and the Carolinas. In 1671 Thomas Batts and Robert Fallam crossed the Blue Ridge and traveled to the western edge of the Great Valley. In 1673 another party led by James Needham reached the present state of Tennessee. The most complete account of these western travels was left by the controversial German immigrant John Lederer.[2]

In the 1660's John Lederer arrived in Virginia from Germany. He either possessed influential friends or displayed exceptional ability, for he quickly came to the attention of Governor William Berkeley. The royal governor, who was involved in the Indian trade, definitely sponsored Lederer's second western journey and perhaps the other two.[3] The first trip lasted only two weeks in March, 1669, but as a result the German probably became the first white to see the Blue Ridge in present-day Madison County, Virginia. Lederer must have found his first excursion enjoyable because he quickly made two other trips. The third journey was the shorter one. On August 20, 1670, he left the falls of the Rappahannock River with ten whites, including a certain "Colonel Catlett," and five Indians. The party reached the summit of the Blue Ridge and then returned. It was the second trip, however, that carried Lederer south into the Carolina Piedmont. In May, 1670, the German and a party of twenty-one Europeans and five Indians left the falls of the James River. The other whites soon became discouraged and abandoned Lederer, but he continued his explorations with an Indian guide. As was the custom of colonial travelers, he usually followed Indian trails. Lederer and the guide

[2] The importance of Lederer's expeditions and his own veracity are an interesting historiographical study. The older authorities tend to underestimate the extent of his travels and question his honesty. The best account of Lederer's travels, which seems to end any dispute about the route of his explorations and which accepts his essential truthfulness, is William P. Cumming, ed., *Discoveries of John Lederer with Unpublished Letters by and about Lederer to Governor John Winthrop, Jr.*, 74–90 et passim.

[3] Alvord and Bidgood, *First Explorations*, 66, 69. Cumming indicates that Berkeley sponsored the last two trips. *Discoveries of Lederer*, viii. Ray A. Billington believes that the royal governor was responsible for all three expeditions. *Western Expansion: A History of the American Frontier*, 80.

traveled south about 250 miles, and not until mid-July did he return to white settlements.[4] Probably because of his association with Governor Berkeley, who was under increasing criticism, Lederer found himself in disfavor in Virginia, and after his third journey he went to Maryland. There he soon made a favorable impression on Sir William Talbot, a member of the Council, and became a naturalized citizen in 1671. Talbot sought to restore his friend's reputation and translated from Latin into English the account of his travels. In 1672 the work was published in London under the title of *The Discoveries of John Lederer, in Three Several Marches from Virginia, to the West of Carolina, and Other Parts of the Continent* . . . .[5]

The German explorer wrote far more concerning his second trip, especially about the period after his white companions had left him, than of his first or third journey. His truthfulness has been doubted. In his trips he referred to having crossed "Savannae" and a large "desert." Lederer may have been merely indicating his reaction to parts of the Piedmont, areas of which were marshy or quite dry and sandy, but his statement that the "Ushery" or Catawba Indians lived near brackish water was not true. The German's story of being asked to join a tribe with the daughter of a "king" or nobleman for a wife also seems highly romantic. His account of the Southern Indians, however, has been recognized as quite valuable.[6]

Lederer devoted a separate section to "the Manners and Customs of the Indians inhabiting the Western parts of Carolina and Virginia." Brief comments regarding the red men were also scattered throughout the journal, and the remarks ranged over many aspects of the Indians' life. The explorer made more comments about native

[4] Cumming, *Discoveries of Lederer*, 19, 33–34. The best general study of the paths used by Southeastern Indians is William E. Myer, "Indian Trails of the Southeast," BAE *Forty-second Annual Report*, 727–857.

[5] Cumming, *Discoveries of Lederer*, 95–107. For bibliographical data on the book, see Clark, *Travels in the Old South*, I, 101–102. For convenience, the Cumming edition in *Discoveries of Lederer*, 1–43, has been used.

[6] *Ibid.*, 10, 23, 31–32, 34–35. Cumming offers this explanation of the "Savanae" and "desert." The best commentary on the Indians visited by Lederer is Douglas L. Rights and W. P. Cumming, "The Indians of Lederer's *Discoveries*," in *ibid.*, 111–26.

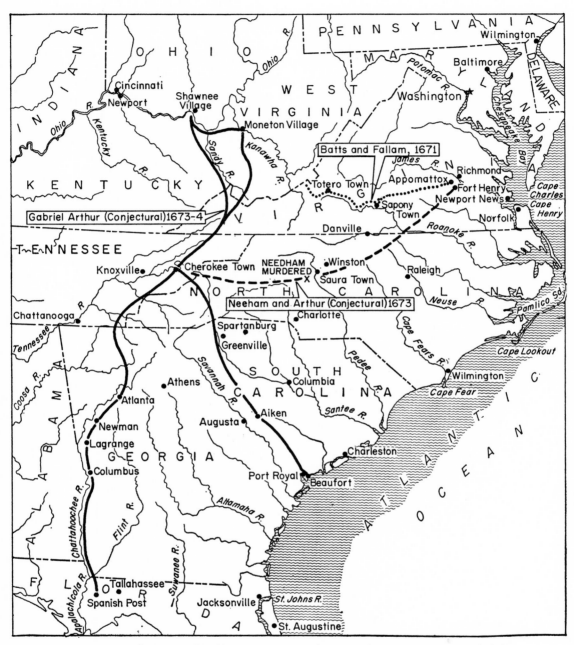

Journeys of Batts and Fallam, 1671; Needham and Arthur, 1673; Gabriel
Arthur, 1673–74

political organization than about any other aspect of the cultures, but he also revealed an interest in warfare, social mores, house types, education, and religion.

The European believed that most of the Indians were ruled by monarchs. Some of these "kings" had great power, and he remarked that among the "Sapony" the people were "slaves, rather than subjects of their king." Only one group, the "Oenock" or Eno, had a democratic form of government. He also noted tribal divisions among the Indians, and reported that as a general rule each tribe had some emblem. For example, he cited the use of a tortoise by the "Sasquesahanaugh." Unlike other travelers who visited the Indians, Lederer was not overly concerned with native warfare. His only comment regarding military affairs was that among the "Oustack" or Yuchi the women fought along with the men. This tale of Amazon-like women was told to Lederer, however, and not reported as witnessed by him. He was quite interested in Indian religion and mythology. He noted that when he and his guides reached the mountains on his first trip, the Indians knelt in worship and told him that the gods were nearby. Elsewhere, he noted that short pieces of straw or reeds were used in a religious ceremony. He thought that the native Americans worshiped "one God, Creator of all things" and that they also had a concept of lesser gods and animal spirits. He noted that villages had a "high priest" and lesser priests for lesser gods. And he reported one Indian myth. The Indians related that long ago they had migrated into the Piedmont and had taught the original inhabitants agriculture and the use of fire. They also believed that four women had been the mothers of all mankind. Therefore the Indians were divided into "four Tribes, distinguished under several names." Unfortunately, Lederer did not indicate which tribe or tribes told him the myth. Regarding the social customs of the Indians, Lederer was unusually perceptive. He noted that it was considered "incest" for a man to marry within his own tribe and that descent was through the mother. He also thought it noteworthy that the tribes did not bury their dead together and that each corpse was wrapped and buried with offerings. Upon the death of important personages captives were slain.[7]

The German was one of several travelers who would comment on the absence of discipline among Indian children. He did not appreciate the lack of parental supervision, for he and his horse were once nearly hit by arrows shot by a mischievous boy. He noted that knowledge was transmitted from father to son and that "emblems or hieroglyphicks" were used to help recall the past. Lederer gave a few meanings of the symbols. For example, a "Stag" meant swiftness, a dog signified fidelity, and a swan meant the English, "alluding to their complexion, and flight over the Sea." In the same passage, the explorer noted the use of knotted cords to indicate numbers and small piles of stones to show numbers killed in battle or the number of people beginning a new settlement. Evidently Lederer was not greatly interested in the everyday life of the Indians, because he said nothing about their food, clothing, or appearance. He did note briefly that the Indians obtained minerals from the "mountains" to make body coloring, and he commented on the houses of the "Oenocks." These homes were usually round in shape and constructed of "watling and plaister." Finally, Lederer noted the similarity of the language spoken by the red men in the area that he visited but indicated that it consisted of several dialects.[8] On the matter of language similarities Lederer was correct in most cases. Of the eighteen groups mentioned by Lederer, nine definitely spoke Siouan and two other groups may have spoken it also. He encountered natives who belonged to the Algonkin, Iroquoian, and Yuchi or Uchean language families.

John Lederer was an intelligent and sympathetic observer of the Southern Piedmont Indians. The only Indian group for which he showed obvious dislike was the "Oenock." Of them he wrote, "They

---

[7] *Ibid.*, 11–30.

[8] *Ibid.*, 10–12, 26–29. On the matter of language affiliation and tribal groupings, see George P. Murdock, *Ethnographic Bibliography of North America*, 120–22, 128; and Driver, *Indian Tribes of North America*, 16, 22, 24, 29, 30. These two works will be used throughout the study on the question of language and tribal affiliations, unless otherwise noted.

are of mean stature and courage, covetous and thievish, industrious to earn a penny; and therefore hire themselves out to their neighbors, who employ them as Carryers or Porters."[9] Usually he had only praise for the red man, and he especially admired the oratorical ability of the Indians. At the end of his *Discoveries*, Lederer offered some advice to other travelers. In his opinion, they should be well stocked with "trading cloth," iron tools, liquor, and "trinkets," and they should always appear courageous.[10] The next Englishmen who ventured into the Virginia Piedmont were certainly courageous, one of them to the point of losing his life while traveling among the Indians.

In 1671 and 1673, Abraham Wood sent explorers across the mountains. Wood was interested in the fur trade and undoubtedly hoped to find new sources of valuable pelts and hides. The first party was led by Captain Thomas Batts and Robert Fallam. They left Fort Henry, the site of present-day Petersburg, Virginia, on the Appomattox River in September, 1671, and crossed the Blue Ridge and the Great Valley before turning back. Batts and Fallam visited the "Sepiny" [Saponi] and the "Totera" Indians of the Piedmont but evidently did not encounter any transmontane red men during the one-month journey. The second party sponsored by Wood, that of James Needham and Gabriel Arthur, did cross the mountains and found the "Tomahitan," probably a part of the Cherokee nation, in the present state of Tennessee. Needham and Arthur left Fort Henry in April, 1673, and Needham returned in September. Arthur was left among the Indians to learn the language. On Needham's return trip to the "Tomahitans," he became involved in a dispute with his guide, who murdered him. Arthur, a prisoner of the "Tomahitans," nevertheless joined three war parties. He was captured by other Indians and soon gained his freedom. He returned to Fort Henry in 1674, but not until he had been ambushed by four Ocaneechi Indians at the site of Needham's murder.[11]

---

[9] Cumming, *Discoveries of Lederer*, 27.
[10] *Ibid.*, 14, 41–42.
[11] Alvord and Bidgood, *First Explorations*, 70–89, 210–26.

The material regarding the Indians encountered by Wood's two parties is sparse. The Batts-Fallam party merely remarked that the Saponi welcomed them with food and by firing guns and that the Totera gave them a similar salute as they left. Fallam, who kept a brief journal of the expedition, commented that the gesture of the Totera Indians was "more than usual." James Needham kept a journal of his explorations, but it is not known to exist today. In 1674, however, Abraham Wood wrote a letter concerning the journey and included several of the party's observations regarding the Indians. The "Tomahitans" were very interested in their visitors, and Wood reported that the explorers and their native guide were placed on a scaffold so that the "people might stand and gaze at them and not offend them by theire throng." The red men made war with their neighbors, and their village was defensively situated. It was located on a high bluff on the river and surrounded on the land sides by twelve-foot walls "with parrapits to defend the walls and offend theire enemies which men stand on to fight." The town measured "300 paces over" and 150 large canoes were drawn up before it. Wood also indicated some of the foodstuffs of the natives; he mentioned corn, fish, buffalo, and "flesh." The Englishmen were not the first Europeans to have contact with the "Tomahitans," for the Indians had about sixty guns which were not of English manufacture. They told of "a white people which have long beards and whiskers and weares clothing" and "have a bell which is six foot over which they ring morning and evening . . . ." Furthermore, the Indians reported that on one occasion they had sent twenty men to trade with the whites, who undoubtedly were Spaniards, but instead of trading, the Europeans had killed and captured the men.[12]

Although the comments concerning the native Americans by the adventurers from Virginia are not as full as would be desired, these men were among the first Europeans to encounter several of the tribes. Their efforts greatly expanded knowledge of the Piedmont

[12] *Ibid.*, 185, 193, 212–14. Buffalo were not named, but they must have been the source of the "many hornes like bulls hornes."

and the trans-Appalachian regions of Virginia and the Carolinas. Meanwhile, other Englishmen were adding to the world's knowledge of the Carolina coast and its inhabitants. Behind these voyages of the 1660's was the desire of the Carolina Proprietors to learn more of the region they proposed to settle.[13]

Even before the Proprietors of Carolina had a clear claim to their colony an expedition was sent to explore the coastline. About 1660 an unsuccessful attempt had been made by some New Englanders to settle at Cape Fear, but detailed information regarding the region was lacking. Therefore, in 1663 Peter Colleton and a "Colonel Modiford" commissioned William Hilton to discover a suitable site for a proposed colony of Barbadians on the mainland.[14] Hilton already had some knowledge of the Carolina coast for in 1662 he had sailed from New England to Cape Fear.[15] Now he was to explore the area farther south. On August 10, Hilton left Barbados in the ship *Adventurer* and reached the continent in a fortnight. Sailing northward he contacted the first Indians near Port Royal and after freeing some English prisoners of the Indians, he moved up the coast. After spending some time among the Indians at Cape Fear he sailed for Barbados in December. Because of a lack of interest on the part of the Proprietors, nothing came of the proposals of Colleton and Modiford to settle Carolina.[16]

In 1664 a "Relation" of Hilton's activities was published in

[13] The explorations of Lederer, Batts-Fallam, and Needham-Arthur influenced the Carolina Proprietors, especially Lord Ashley. The explorations of Lederer were especially influential in the cartography of the seventeenth and eighteenth centuries. William P. Cumming has found thirty-three maps based at least partly on the German's findings. "Geographical Misconceptions of the Southeast in the Cartography of the Seventeenth and Eighteenth Centuries," *Journal of Southern History*, Vol. IV (Nov., 1938), 489–90.

[14] For a discussion of the conflicting claims to Carolina, see Edward McCrady, *History of South Carolina under the Proprietary Government, 1670–1719*, 54–79. The relationship of Colleton and Modiford to the Proprietors is not known.

[15] William Hilton, "The Relacon of the Late Discovery made in Florida." Royal Society Classified Papers. Vol. VII, Pt. 1. Photostat. Manuscript Division of the Library of Congress.

[16] William Hilton, "A Relation of a Discovery Lately Made on the Coast of Florida, (From Lat. 31 to 33 Deg. 45 Min. North-Lat., 1663)," in William A. Courtenay, ed., *Genesis of South Carolina, 1562–1670*, 1–40.

London, and it revealed the author's considerable interest in as well as his apprehension toward the red men along the Carolina coast. The Indians that Hilton visited were already familiar with Europeans. He reported that the "Port Royal" Indians, probably a part of the Cusbo tribe, willingly came aboard the *Adventurer* and that they knew a few Spanish words such as "Capptian" and "Adeus." Later, he noted that Catawbas at Cape Fear were raising "English" cattle and swine and believed that they had acquired their stock from a settlement of New Englanders a few years before.[17]

The "Relation" also indicated other aspects of the native culture. Hilton observed that the houses of the "Port Royal" Indians were shaped like a "Dove-house" and were about two hundred feet long with twelve-foot walls. The exterior of each was covered with palmetto leaves. He also noted several smaller houses, one of which he believed to have been a "Sentinel-house." The foods of the Indians, which they willingly shared, were corn, pumpkins, melons, fruits, including grapes, figs and peaches, and wildlife such as venison and fish. He believed the Indians were able to harvest more than one crop of corn each year despite the fact that they farmed "the worst Land, because they cannot cut down the Timber in the best . . . ." Hilton also gave some hint of the crafts of the natives. He casually mentioned seeing an Indian basket at Port Royal and "mats," "pots, platters, and spoons" among the Cape Fear Indians.[18]

Hilton was cautious and somewhat fearful in his contacts with the native Americans. Early in the "Relation" he mentioned suspecting treachery on the part of the Indians. At Cape Fear when the long boat from the *Adventurer* was moving along the shore an arrow was shot at it. No one was hurt, but when the party went ashore they saw an Indian apparently trying to approach unseen and fired at him. The

---

[17] Hilton, "Relation," 4, 26–27. For bibliographical data on the book, see Clark, *Travels in the Old South*, I, 91.

[18] Hilton, "Relation," 7–8, 13, 22. It should be noted that the figs and peaches that the Indians were growing were not native to North America but were further evidence of their earlier contact with Europeans. For a list of native plants grown by North American Indians, see Driver, *Indians of North America*, 43–44.

explorers' handling of the situation did not improve the Indians' opinion of Europeans. When the English discovered the canoe of the hostile Indian, they destroyed it, together with his house and its contents. The Europeans also probably offended the Indians by rejecting their peace offering. Hilton reported that the natives tried to make amends by giving the Englishmen "two very handsom young *Indian* women, the tallest that we have seen in this Countrey; which we supposed to be the Kings Daughters, or persons of some great account amongst them."[19] The whites did not accept the "noble" offering, but did take an Indian called "Shadoo" to Barbados.[20]

Despite his caution, Hilton believed that the Indians were friendly. The "Relation" was written and published to promote Carolina, and the author certainly did not wish to frighten prospective settlers. The Carolina Proprietors failed to act on the suggestions of Hilton's sponsors, but the glowing description of the natural resources of the region could not but aid in increasing the desire to colonize it.

Two years after Hilton's voyage a group of settlers from Barbados did arrive in the Carolinas. In November, 1665, the colonists landed at the mouth of the Cape Fear River. Sir John Yeamans had been appointed governor of the colony to be known as the County of Clarendon, but he soon returned to Barbados. Before he left, however, he instructed Robert Sandford, clerk and register of the county, to explore the coastline to the south. Because of the lack of a suitable vessel, Sandford was delayed in his explorations until the middle of 1666. On June 16 of that year, Sandford and twenty other men left Cape Fear in a sloop and a shallop. For one month the party explored the coast as far south as Port Royal. Upon his return, Sandford lavishly praised the area he had seen. His account contained less on the wildlife than Hilton's, but Sandford appeared to have been more curious and less frightened of the Indians. Much of his sojourn was spent in the company of natives who were consistently friendly.[21]

[19] Hilton, "Relation," 20–24.

[20] Hilton did not mention the incident, but see Robert Sandford, "A Relation of a Voyage on the Coast of the Province of Carolina . . . Begun 14th June, 1666," in Courtenay, *Genesis*, 54, 60.

The first red men encountered by the Sandford party were two Edisto Indians who came aboard the sloop on June 22. On the next day Sandford landed and, following his instructions, took formal possession of the land from 36° north to 29° south and west to the Pacific. Soon the Europeans resumed their explorations and shortly afterwards they met the Edisto Indian Shadoo whom Hilton had taken to Barbados. Shadoo wanted some of the whites to visit his village, and after taking the precaution of keeping some Indians on board the vessel as guarantees for the men's safety, Sandford permitted four gentlemen to accompany Shadoo. The "Casique" of the village was absent, but the whites were entertained by his wife. Sandford was so pleased with the courtesy of the Indians that he decided to visit the town. He noted that on the way the natives would not permit him to wade the creeks and marshes. They carried him across. At the village, Sandford and Captain George Cary were conducted to a "large house of a Circular forme (their generall house of State)." The interior of the house was encircled by a bench with a "high seat" opposite the entrance and a fire in the center.[22]

Sandford and Cary were welcomed with presents of "skins." Before he left, Sandford inspected the town. He noted that it was located among several "Maiz" fields.

Before the Doore of their State-house is a spacious walke rowed with trees on both sides tall & full branched not unlike to Elms which serves for the Exercise and recreation of the men who by Couple runn after a marble bowle troled out alternatively by themselves whith six foote staves in their hands which they tosse after the bowle in their race, and according to the laying of these staves wine or loose the beeds they contend for; an exercise approveable enough in the winter but somewhat too violent (meethought) for that season and noon time of the day.[23]

---

[21] *Ibid.*, 41–84 and McCrady, *Proprietary Government*, 79–81. McCrady's belief that the region south of Cape Fear was unknown to the Yeamans' party may be incorrect. Hilton's "Relation" had already been published, and Sandford definitely knew of Hilton's taking an Indian to Barbados.

[22] Sandford, "Relation," 51–56.

[23] *Ibid.*, 57.

The game witnessed was one version of chunkey, a very popular form of amusement among the Southeastern Indians. Sandford also saw another field for the young people's recreational use.

On June 27 the expedition left the Edisto and after further explorations in the area, sailed southward. Early in July Sandford encountered the Indians of Port Royal. He was impressed with the richness of the soil and was amazed that grapes grew abundantly among many weeds and bushes. He noted that the native Americans had adopted a hair style learned from Spanish missionaries. He thought that the reason for the Indians continued courtesy was each tribe's desire to prove itself friendlier than any other. On July 7 the English hoped to begin their voyage back to Cape Fear, but they were delayed a short time. A leader of some of the Port Royal Indians asked Sandford to take his nephew with him so that the youth could learn English. One of the whites, Henry Woodward, whom Sandford described as a "Chirurgeon," or surgeon, offered to remain among the red men to learn their language. The Indians were highly pleased with the offer and gave Woodward a field of corn and the sister of the young man who was going with the English.[24]

On his return voyage, Sandford noted an excellent harbor, but adverse winds prevented his entering it. He did give the name "Ashley" to one of the rivers that emptied into the harbor. On July 12, 1666, the Sandford expedition returned to the Cape Fear settlement, and its leader presented the colonists with profuse descriptions of the region he had seen. The Barbadian colony on the Cape Fear River soon disappeared, but the efforts of William Hilton and Robert Sandford had the desired effect, and within a few years permanent settlement of the Carolina grant was achieved.[25]

Henry Woodward, who remained with the Indians of Port Royal in 1666, spent much of his life among the red men of South Carolina. Shortly after Sandford's departure the surgeon was cap-

[24] *Ibid.*, 77–80.
[25] *Ibid.*, 84, and McCrady, *Proprietary Government*, 92–93.

tured by Spaniards and taken to St. Augustine. There he professed Roman Catholicism and gained the freedom of the town. In 1668 he was rescued by a buccaneer, Robert Searles. He was shipwrecked on Nevis in 1669 and later in the same year joined the colonists under William Sayle who settled South Carolina. In 1674 Woodward became the agent of the Earl of Shaftesbury and visited the Westo Indians. As a result of this expedition, important trade began between the colony and the tribe. In the early 1680's, however, a controversy arose over the Indian trade policy of South Carolina, and Woodward fell into temporary disgrace. Later he played a vital role in establishing trade relations with the Lower Creeks.[26]

The best account that Woodward left of his visits with Indians concerned the 1674 journey to the Westos. Some Westos came to the plantation of the Earl of Shaftesbury near Charles-Town and after some difficulty made their desire known. Woodward seemingly did not understand the language of the Westos, for he reported that he realized that they wanted to establish trade when he saw an Indian drawing a tree, "the effigies of a bever, a man, on horseback and guns, Intimating thereby as I suppose, their desire for freindship [*sic*] and commerse w[i]th us." With the Indians as guides, the Englishman went to visit Westo villages on the Savannah River. Although the purpose of the trip was to secure the Westo trade, Woodward presented evidence that the natives already had commerce with Europeans. Upon his entrance into a large village he was given a noisy welcome. The Westos shouted and fired "a volley of fifty or sixty small arms." He believed that the Indians had guns, ammunition, and

---

[26] For contemporary criticism of the Indian trade, which was controlled by a few Englishmen including Woodward, see Thomas Newe, "Letters, 1682," in Alexander S. Salley, ed., *Narratives of Early Carolina, 1650–1708*, 182–83. For Woodward, see J. W. Barnwell, "Dr. Henry Woodward, the First English Settler in South Carolina, and Some of His Descendants," *South Carolina Historical and Genealogical Magazine*, Vol. VII (Jan., 1907), 29–41; and Walter A. Harris, *Here the Creeks Sat Down*, 63–143 *et passim*. The latter work should be used with extreme caution. Harris seemingly located most of the material relating to Woodward but went beyond normal historical standards in re-creating Woodward's thoughts and motives.

cloth obtained "from the northward," probably Virginia, by trading pelts and slaves.[27]

Woodward also noted that many canoes were drawn up before the village which was situated on the bank of the river and was fortified with a palisade. The walls that completely encircled the town were doubled on the land side. He described the village and its houses as being "built in a confused maner, consisting of many long houses whose sides and tops are both artifitially done w[i]th barke, upon the tops of most wherof fastened the ends of long poles hang the locks of haire of Indians that they have slaine." He was taken to the chief's house, but so many Indians wanted to see the stranger that the top of the house had to be removed to permit viewing. After a visit of ten days Woodward left the Indian town. During his stay, the Westos were visited by a party of "Savana" Indians, a wandering group of Shawnees who came to trade. The Indians could not understand each other, but the commerce was carried on by signs. Dr. Woodward was successful in opening trade with the Westos. He ended his account with the comment that during March of the next year he expected a trading party to bring deerskins, furs and "young slaves."[28]

Desire for trade with the Indians and discovery of suitable locations for British colonies were the primary motives behind the exploring of the 1660's and 1670's. From records left by the courageous whites, it is apparent that they were not initially interested in the native Americans and their culture. Europeans frequently commented on the Indians, but their observations were usually brief, concerned only with the superficial aspects of native life.

In the half-century following the Stuart Restoration, several men who were not interested in exploring new territory or opening new markets for British goods reported contact with the Southeastern

[27] "A Faithfull Relation of my Westoe Voiage by Henry Woodward, 1674," in Salley, *Narratives*, 128–34. The identity of the Westos has been a subject of controversy. John T. Juricek recently concluded that the Westos were not a single tribe but a combination of Indian groups displaced by European movement into the Southeast. "The Westo Indians," *Ethnohistory*, Vol. XI (Spring, 1964), 134–73.

[28] Woodward, "Faithfull Relation," 132–34.

Indians. Some of these meetings were intentional but most were accidental. The encounters were usually transitory. The resulting accounts reveal a common reluctance or disinterest in understanding the complexities of native civilization by the British.

III

Colonists and Travelers
Among the Coastal Indians, 1670–1719

IN 1669 the Proprietors of Carolina began a determined effort to colonize their grant, and in the next year William Sayle, first governor of South Carolina, led a group of settlers from England, Ireland, Barbados, and perhaps Bermuda to the colony. In March, the English landed at Bull's Island but soon moved to Port Royal, which had been designated as the site for settlement. In April the colonists moved a short distance up the Ashley River and located at a place they named "Albemarle Point." The Europeans were welcomed by the "Kiawha" Indians; indeed, the red men were instrumental in showing the way to the rich land on the Ashley. Despite internal conflict over the powers of the officials and problems arising from the instructions of the Proprietors, who usually had little knowledge of actual conditions in the colony, by 1710 South Carolina had a population of more than five thousand whites. During the forty-year period, relations between the Carolinians and the native Americans were generally peaceful.

Nicholas Carteret, who apparently was a member of the Sayle party in 1670, related that the Indians were very friendly to the whites. The English were made welcome by the Indians, who stroked the shoulders of the Europeans. At "Sowee," the present Sewee Bay of Bull's Island, Governor Sayle was carried into the "Hutt Pallace" of the local chieftain. The governor also commented on the general amity of the natives but noted that there were exceptions. A small party of the Europeans was fired on "with small shot" by some Indians. He went on to state that he believed that the hostilities were due to Spanish, who were active among the Carolina Indians. One reason for the friendliness of the Indians may have been their desire for protection against Spanish Indians and the Westos, an aggressive tribe on the Savannah River.[1]

Almost all of the comments of Sayle and Carteret regarding the natives dealt with their reaction to the strangers. Carteret did note that the Indian women wore "mosse roabs," and he listed some of the native foods. He seemed intrigued by the fact that the red men ate hickory nuts in addition to venison and fish.[2] A lack of interest in the culture of the American Indian was typical of the early settlers of South Carolina, and it continued for several years. In 1687 a "Captain Dunlop" made a trip from Charles-Town to St. Catherine's Island, but despite his visits to several native towns with Indian guides, he made no comment on the Indians.[3] Two accounts dating from the early period did contain material on the Indian civilization. Both of them were written in the early 1680's, one by "R.F." and the other by "T.A.," who was almost certainly Thomas Ashe.

In 1680 Thomas Ashe was clerk of the *Richmond*, a vessel which carried a group of Huguenots to South Carolina. Two years later he returned to England and promptly published a promotional tract praising the new colony. In his short pamphlet Ashe devoted a few pages to the Indians and touched on several aspects of their life. He noted that the natives of South Carolina had a "Deep Chestnut Colour" and that they painted their faces. Of their crafts, he stated that they made baskets, bows, and arrows of reeds with stone or fishbone points. Although he gave no details, Ashe did comment that the

[1] "Mr. Carteret's Relation of their Planting at Ashley River '70," and "Letter of Governor Sayle and Council, Albemarle Point, Sep[tembe]r 9th, 1670," in Salley, *Narratives*, 116–20, 122–23.

[2] Carteret, "Relation," 117.

[3] "Capt. Dunlop's Voyage to the Southward, 1687," *South Carolina Historical and Genealogical Magazine*, Vol. XXX (July, 1929), 127–33.

red men were divided into nations. Perhaps his best observations dealt with the religion of the Indians. After indicating that they worshiped the sun and the moon, he stated: "At the Appearance of the New Moon I have observed them with open extended Arms[,] then folded, with inclined Bodies, to make their Adorations with much Ardency and Passion . . . ." The clerk also believed that the native Americans had been quite helpful to the whites, and in a discussion of the hygiene of the colony noted that the Indians lived to a very old age.[4]

About the same time that Thomas Ashe's account appeared, "R.F." wrote "The Present State of Carolina, with Advice to the Settlers."[5] Much of the material regarding the Indians in it related to locations of tribes and numbers of warriors. "R.F." emphasized the small size of Indian groups in Carolina. Except for the large tribes of Tuscaroras and Westos, he believed that no group had more than "Fifty Bowmen." In describing the political organization of the Indians, the author of the "Present State" applied European terms to the leaders of the natives. He stated that although the Westos had only "Kings," the Tuscaroras were ruled by a "Sagamore, or great Emperor of many Kings." The manner of living of the red man also drew the attention of the writer. Some, but not all, of the Indians lived in villages. Of the latter, he wrote that they were found "in straggling Plantations; often removing for the better convenience of Hunting, for that [is] their general Exercise, and a great part of their Maintainace [*sic*]." Except for this comment, "R.F." made no mention of the Indians' food or their means of acquiring it. He believed that the English had no reason to fear that the natives would become very numerous and powerful because the women practiced birth control. He reported that at about the age of twenty-seven women ate the root of some plant and became sterile. They had been doing this for generations and would not cease, although the writer thought some

[4] *Carolina; or a Description of the Present State of that Country, and the Natural Excellencies Thereof* . . . , in Bartholomew R. Carroll, ed., *Historical Collections of South Carolina; . . . from Its First Discovery to . . . 1776*, II, 59–84.

[5] Transcript. Manuscript Division of the Library of Congress. There is a note on the transcript that it is a copy of a book published in London in 1682.

attempts had been made to prevent the practice. "R.F." did not report the birth control custom from his own observations but heard it from a "worthy and knowable person."[6]

At least one well-known figure in the early history of the Carolinas did report on the Indians. This was John Archdale. In 1707 *A New Description of that Fertile and Pleasant Province of Carolina with a Brief Account of Its Discovery. Settling, and the Government thereof at This Time. With Several Remarkable Passages of Divine Providence during My Time, By John Archdale: Late Governor of the Same* was published in London.[7] The book was essentially an attempt to show God's assistance to man and to justify the two administrations of its controversial author. Archdale was a Quaker and considered himself one of the Proprietors of Carolina. The claim was disputed, but in 1682 he was sent to the Albemarle settlements in the northern portion of the province to collect quit rents. He remained in the colony for about one year and then returned to England. In 1694 he was commissioned governor of the southern colony in Carolina, but he did not arrive in Charles-Town until the next year. Most of his two-year administration in South Carolina centered on the struggle over the rights of the Quaker and Huguenot dissenters. After returning to England, Archdale was elected to Parliament, but the House of Commons declined to seat him when he refused to take the oath of loyalty because of his Quaker principles. He remained interested in the Carolinas, but he did not return to America.

One of Archdale's primary purposes was to show that much of the progress made in Carolina was due to the "divine providence" of God. His strong religious belief was apparent in his comments about Indians. Archdale stated that English settlement had been made easier because God had permitted the red men to exterminate themselves by constant warfare and by disease, especially "a Consumption." The defense of his administration also appeared in observations regarding the native Americans. Archdale believed that he had pre-

[6] *Ibid.*
[7] In Carroll, *Historical Collections*, II, 85–120.

vented war between two tribes. Two Indians became drunk on rum, argued, and one killed the other. The former governor thought that war would have resulted had he not captured and executed the murderer. Archdale had to admire the courage of the condemned man, who refused to be tied to a tree and stood free, awaiting execution by shooting.[8]

Archdale made relatively few comments concerning the Indians. He believed that their "Tawny" color was a result of sunlight and a practice of oiling their bodies. He wrote that "they are generally very straight Bodied, and Comely in person, and quick of Apprehension." He also recognized the natives' skill in hunting. Indians killed deer not only for the skins, which they traded to the Europeans, but also for the venison, which they sold cheaply. Whites could also purchase a "wild Turky of 40 pounds for the Value of two Pence *Engl.* Value." The remarks on the cheapness of meat may have been intended to promote immigration to the colony as much as to reflect the author's praise of the natives' hunting skills.[9]

On the whole, the former governor believed that his policy towards the natives was successful. He noted that some of the Indians at Cape Fear desired English protection from slavers. He warned them that to secure English support they would have to reciprocate. He felt justified when a short time later a ship was wrecked on the coast and the Indians fed and cared for the survivors. He also freely offered advice on means of improving relations with the Indians. He stressed the need for fairness in dealing with them and for their conversion to Christianity.[10]

The emphasis on missionary activity among the Indians was not unique to Archdale. When the former governor wrote his account, the Venerable Society for the Propagation of the Gospel in Foreign

---

[8] *Ibid.*, 88–90, 94–95.

[9] *Ibid.*, 93–94.

[10] *Ibid.*, 94, 98–99, 108–109. McCrady questioned the fairness of Archdale's administration. He noted that there were differences in the punishments given whites and Indians for the same crimes and that the Indians were forced to pay tribute to the Europeans. *Proprietary Government*, 285.

Parts had only recently been organized, and one of its early goals was to work among heathen Indians and Negroes. In 1702, the year after the society was founded, it sent the Reverend Mr. Samuel Thomas to South Carolina to labor among the Yamassee Indians. Governor Sir Nathaniel Johnson thought it best that Thomas confine his efforts to the English, and the missionary became the minister at Goose Creek.[11]

In 1706 the Reverend Mr. Francis Le Jau was sent to replace Thomas, who had died the year before. In addition to his work among the English settlers at Goose Creek, Le Jau converted and baptized some of the planters' Negro and Indian slaves and had some contact with free Indians.[12] In reports to his superiors in London, Le Jau commented upon the Indians and criticized the Europeans who had the most contact with the natives. The Anglican minister believed that white traders deliberately provoked warfare in order to secure more slaves and that they stoutly opposed missionary efforts among the red men. He thought that Indians wanted to learn of Christianity. They were "a good sort of people" but were being corrupted. Perhaps to emphasize the need for more missionaries, he indicated that the morals of the natives had suffered from contact with Europeans.[13]

With his interest in converting Indians, it seemed natural that he was attracted to native religious practices. He believed that there were definite parallels between the Indians' religion and that of the Jews. In 1708 the missionary wrote that "he observes among some of the nations of the Indians several old Legal Ceremonies, such as Circumcision, the feast, and a kind of offering of first fruits when their

[11] *Ibid.*, 340; Charles F. Pascoe, *Two Hundred Years of the S. P. G.: An Historical Account of the Society for the Propagation of the Gospel in Foreign Parts, 1701–1900*, chap. i; and Evarts B. Greene, "The Anglican Outlook on the American Colonies in the Early Eighteenth Century," *American Historical Review*, Vol. XX (Oct., 1914), 71, 73.

[12] Pascoe, *Two Hundred Years of the S. P. G.*, 849; Edward McCrady, *History of South Carolina under the Royal Government, 1719–1776*, 49, 197; and David Humphreys, *Historical Account of the Incorporated Society for the Propagation of the Gospel in Foreign Parts . . . to the Year 1728*, I, viii.

[13] Francis Le Jau, "Letters, Sept. 15, Nov. 15, 1708; Feb. 18, 1708/09; Mar. 22, 1708/09; Aug. 5, 1709." "Journals of the Proceedings of the S. P. G., 1701–1900." Vol. I, Pt. 2. Photostat. Manuscript Division of the Library of Congress. Frank J. Klingberg has edited the letters of Le Jau in *Carolina Chronicle of Dr. Francis Le Jau, 1706–1717.*

corn is ripe . . . ." In other letters Le Jau made additional references to circumcision among the natives.[14] Two years later the missionary attended a dance of the neighboring "Ittiwan" or Etiwan Indians, members of the Cusabo tribal family, on the parish glebe land. Le Jau questioned the natives when he noted that there were no women present. The Indians replied that women were forbidden to participate because man had been made first and that woman had been fashioned from a man's rib. Later, the Englishman reported witnessing another dance. In October, 1711, he said, "I went to see how our Ittiwan Indians kept one of their Solemn Festivalls, I saw abt. *40* of them trimd painted and dress'd in their fineryes Coming from the Woods near a little hut Supported upon Pillars all painted and adorned." As was his custom, the Anglican questioned an Indian concerning the meaning of the dance. He was told by "Capt. George," a native, that the "hut" represented a ship and that three young men who led the dance represented an old man's sons. These comments led Le Jau to conclude that the Indians had a tradition of "Noah's Ark and his 3 Sons." The minister never elaborated on his emerging theory that the natives of the New World and the Jewish people might be connected in some manner, but the suspicion was apparent. The possibility that the religious beliefs of the Indians might have been influenced by Spanish and English Christians evidently never occurred to him.[15]

Throughout his life, the minister retained his interest in the Indian and the need for missionary work among the heathen. About a year and a half before his death in 1717 he questioned one "Kirke," "an Ingenious Artist," concerning the Indians of Virginia. The artist thought the Virginia natives to be a "very Brutish Sort of people," but Le Jau still stressed the need of missionaries to learn the "heathen" language and work for their salvation. Some effort had been made to learn the "heathen" language, for in 1708 Le Jau sent to his sponsors

[14] Le Jau, "Letters, Sept. 11 and 18, 1708," in "Journals of the Proceedings," Vol. I, Pt. 2; and Le Jau, *Carolina Chronicle,* 45, 68, 73, 80, 176.

[15] *Ibid.,* 68, 105–106. For the appearance and development of this theory of the origin of the Indians, see Lee E. Huddleston, *Origins of the American Indians: European Concepts, 1492–1729,* 33–47 *et passim.*

a copy of the Lord's Prayer in the "Savannah tongue." A few years later, one of Le Jau's fellow workers, the Reverend Mr. Ebenezer Taylor, made a disparaging remark about "Savannah" Indians. Taylor wrote in 1711 that "the Savannock Indians are dull and mean, but the Floridas are the same with the Crick Indians, are honest [and] Polite." Despite Le Jau's interest, he was not able to become an Indian missionary and died as parish minister at Goose Creek.[16]

The efforts of all the missionaries of the Venerable Society in the Carolinas were severely hampered by two Indian wars in the early 1700's. In the autumn of 1711 a major Indian uprising began in North Carolina. The Tuscaroras, alarmed by European encroachment on their lands and perhaps encouraged by the civil strife within the colony, began a widespread attack upon the English. The worst massacres took place on September 22, 1711, when more than a hundred whites were killed. In 1713, North Carolina, with the aid of Virginia and South Carolina, achieved victory over the Tuscaroras. That their efforts among all of the Carolina Indians were greatly handicapped by the Tuscarora War was apparent in the missionaries' letters to the directors of the society.[17] In 1713 officials in London learned that one of the missionaries, the Reverend Mr. Giles Rainsfold, had been captured by Indians but had escaped unharmed. At the same meeting of the society's governing body, instructions were given for educating "Northern Indians," and the society soon concentrated its work upon the Iroquois.[18] The Venerable Society did not withdraw from the Carolinas but began to take a greater interest in the Negro slaves. The warfare of 1711–1713 with the Tuscaroras of North Carolina and in 1715–1716 with the Yamassees and their allies in South Carolina apparently ended the society's work among the Carolina Indians. More-

---

[16] Le Jau, *Carolina Chronicle*, 175–76; Le Jau, "Letters, Sept. 11 and 18, 1708," in "Journals of the Proceedings," Vol. I, Pt. 2; and Ebenezer Taylor, "Letter, Feb. 9, 1710/11," *ibid.*

[17] For example, see the letters read at the meeting of October 12, 1712. "Journals of the Proceedings of the S. P. G., 1701–1900." Vol. II. Photostat. Manuscript Division of the Library of Congress.

[18] Meeting of October 9, 1713, *ibid.*; and Humphreys, *Historical Account*, 276–311. The Society's efforts among the Iroquois also failed.

over, if the opinion of the secretary of the society, David Humphreys, was shared by any large number of the directors, they probably had little real hope of success. Humphreys thought that the Indians of North America, unlike those of Mexico and Peru, were "utter barbarians" who "knew nothing of Morality or the Common Decencies of human life." The withdrawal of the Venerable Society did not end efforts to Christianize the American Indians, but the Carolina Indians were avoided by later missionaries.[19]

During the same decades that the Carolinas were being colonized, several Europeans observed and commented on the Indians in the more settled areas of the older Southern colonies. A Cavalier visitor, a surgeon, and two itinerant Quakers made some observations on the Indians of Tidewater Virginia. Travelers among the natives of Maryland included a Quaker preacher, an indentured servant, and an Englishman who wrote an anonymous account.

Considering the widespread Indian custom of decorating body and weapons with brightly colored designs and figures, it was perhaps not too strange that an English Cavalier with an interest in heraldry was attracted to the practice. John Gibbon, later author of a standard seventeenth-century work on heraldry, spent most of 1659 and part of 1660 in Virginia. Two decades later he publicly recalled two incidents of his American visit. Gibbon warmly complimented his host, Richard Lee I, and took notice of an Indian war dance that he had witnessed. He noted precisely that the natives were painted "Party per Pale Gul. and Sab. from forehead to foot . . . ." He also observed that the warriors' shields were painted with designs and concluded that "Heraldry was ingrafted naturally into the sense of [the] human race." A few other remarks concerning the shouting of the dancers and the drumming also appeared, but they were vague. Gibbon was obviously not as interested in the red men as he was in furthering his pet theory.[20]

[19] *Ibid.*, 81–143, 277–78.
[20] *Introductio ad blasoniam; or, An Essay to a More Correct Blazon in Latine than Formerly Hath Been Used*, 155–57; and Louis B. Wright, *First Gentlemen of Virginia: Intellectual Qualities of the Early Colonial Ruling Class*, 215, 231.

If the occasion for Gibbon's remarks was unique, the qualifications of George Alsop as an author were also highly unusual. In 1658 the twenty-year-old Alsop went to Maryland and for four years worked as an indentured servant of Thomas Stocket of Baltimore County. Sometime between 1662 and 1666 he returned to England, and in 1666 he wrote and published a promotional tract in London. During his stay in America, Alsop visited the "Susquehanock" Indians of Maryland. The Susquehannas, who spoke Iroquoian, normally remained north of Maryland and Virginia, but occasional bands did move into the Southern colonies. Alsop did not indicate where he visited the Indians, although he did state that "they are situated a hundred and odd miles distant from the Christian Plantations of Mary-Land, at the head of a River that runs into the Bay of Chesapike, called by their own name The Susquehanock River . . . ." He was mistaken about the distance from the Chesapeake Bay and the headwaters of the river. Nothing in his writings indicate that he traveled any great distance from white settlements.[21]

As with all things in Maryland, Alsop took a great deal of pride in the local Indians. He stated that all the settlers agreed that the "Susquehanocks" were "the most Noble and Heroick Nation of Indians that dwell upon the confines of America . . . ." He praised the valor and courage of the Maryland natives and was certain that the neighboring tribes were "submissive" to them. Alsop believed that one reason for the success of the "Susquehanocks" was the size of their men, whom he claimed were "seven foot high," a prime example of his exaggeration. Alsop was interested in Indian warfare but took even greater notice of the treatment of prisoners. He reported that the Indians painted their faces and bodies and decorated their hair with the feathers of "Swans." The Englishman's description of the torture of an enemy was vivid and gruesome. The unfortunate captive was tied to a stake and subjected to scalping, burning and searing with

---

[21] "A Character of the Province of Maryland," in Clayton C. Hall, ed., *Narratives of Early Maryland, 1633–1684*, 337–41, 355, 380. Hall deleted the author's "vulgar" language, but a comparison with a 1666 edition revealed no changes regarding the Indians.

45

"pieces of Iron, and barrels of old Guns, which they made red hot," and finally dismemberment. Alsop admired the courage of the condemned man, who taunted his tormentors with tales of his deeds until dead. The European also related that the Indian warriors ate parts of the slain man, but he had the insight to recognize that human flesh was not a part of the natives' "common dyet." This was ceremonial cannibalism, wherein the participant sought to gain supernatural power from the dead warrior. The practice was widespread in North America.[22]

Alsop's revulsion at the inhumane treatment of captives may have helped him reach the conclusion that the only deity of the red man was the "Devil." Indeed, he wrote that the fear of the Devil was so great among Indians that every four years they sacrificed a child to him. He had little to say of the native religion, believing that "their Rites and Ceremonies, they are so absurd and ridiculous, that its almost a sin to name them." Without conceding any religious basis to their burial customs, he noted that the Indians interred corpses in a sitting position facing west and that food, clothing, and weapons were placed in the grave. Bear skins were worn as a sign of mourning.[23]

Some of the best comments in *A Character of the Province of Mary-Land* concerned the mundane activities of the Indians. Early in the work, Alsop noted that the Indians often traded venison and pelts to whites. In a letter to a friend, he characterized the Indian homes as "little small Bark-Cottages," and elsewhere he indicated that the long, low houses were placed in an irregular fashion within palisades. The appearance of the red men also attracted his attention. He stated that men, women, and children wore very little clothing. Besides habitually painting their faces, some of them had pictures of animals and of the "devil" tattooed on their bodies. The "Susquehanock" women drew strong praise from the Englishman. Besides being "very well featured," they made good wives and did not try to dominate their hus-

---

[22] *Ibid.*, 365–69, 377.
[23] *Ibid.*, 369–70. Driver indicates that human sacrifice was not found in this area. *Indians of North America*, 378.

bands. Then Alsop contradicted an earlier statement by remarking that the women did not "alter their bodies by their dying, painting, and cutting themselves." The marriage ceremony was a simple exchange of gifts, but the men were very faithful. This may have been because the women took care of the house, farmed, and even carried game killed by the men home from the forest. Alsop believed that Purchas was incorrect in stating that the natives of America were governed by monarchies. "Anarchy" was a more precise term in his opinion. Regarding the language of the Indians, Alsop made no comment except to note the vast diversity of native tongues.[24]

Another Englishman who spent some time in the colonies, Thomas Glover, also remarked on the multitude of Indian languages. Alsop would have agreed with Glover's statement that "almost every [Indian] Town differs in language." Although Glover related one fantastic story about a "half-fish" and "half-man" that he found in the Rappahannock River, in comparison to Alsop he usually wrote clearly and simply. Glover, a surgeon, spent a few years in Virginia, and in March, 1676, his description of Virginia and its native and transplanted inhabitants was read at a meeting of the Royal Society in London. Glover seems to have been unusually interested in the Indian, because approximately one-fifth of his communication concerned the red men. He touched on many aspects of Indian culture but gave few details. Indeed, he did not identify the native Americans but merely divided them between Virginia and Maryland when he indicated their population. He believed that the natives of Virginia had declined greatly in numbers and said that because of warfare the Maryland Indians would also become fewer.[25]

Whatever the identity of the Indians in the writings of Glover, they were not Alsop's "Susquehanocks." While the "Susquehanocks" lived in long, low houses, the Virginia Indians that Glover observed

[24] Alsop, "Character," 345–47, 365–77.
[25] Thomas Glover, *Account of Virginia, Its Scituation* [*sic*], *Temperature, Productions, Inhabitants and Their Manner of Planting and Ordering Tobacco, Etc. . . . .*, 21–22. By "language," both Alsop and Glover meant what anthropologists refer to as "dialects."

built cone-shaped houses of poles gathered at the top and covered with bark. Glover also reported that the natives burned their dead and kept the ashes in their homes. Alsop believed "Anarchy" characterized Indian life, but Glover took the more conventional view that they were governed by kings. The surgeon felt that he knew little of the Indians' religion, but he did relate that a "priest" had "caused" rain by chanting. He noted the offering of the first slain deer as a sacrifice. Both Glover and Alsop praised the physical appearance of the Indian and both commented on his having no scruples against eating any wild animal.[26]

The aspects of Indian civilization dealt with by Glover were not always the same as those selected by Alsop. The Virginia surgeon was more aware of the effect of the European on the natives. He noted that the Indians had adopted the use of hooks and lines in fishing, but before white contact they had fished with a torch at night. Evidently the Indians had used a spear or bow and arrow to secure the fish, but Glover was silent on this point. Elsewhere, he indicated that the native Americans had at least some knowledge of Christianity. He was told by some of them that the Christian God was "good," but that theirs was "an angry God, [who] oftentimes beats them." It was perhaps natural that the surgeon was interested in medical practices of the Indians. The medicines of the red men were mainly herbal "decoctions," evidently used to aid difficult breathing and to cause the patient to perspire. Glover believed that they had a medicine to cure snake bites, and he noted that neither purging nor bleeding was used by the Indians.[27] Although they might have wondered at the names of the strange red men, the members of the Royal Society who attended the meeting in March, 1676, must have gone away with a fairly clear idea of some of the Indians of Virginia.

Another Englishman who visited the American Indians left an account of his observations, but his identity is unknown. Between October, 1705, and October, 1706, he traveled in Maryland, and later

[26] *Ibid.*, 21–25; and Alsop, "Character," 365–66, 369.
[27] Glover, *Account of Virginia*, 23–27.

Stone Pipe of an Indian Preparing to Throw a "Chunkey"
Stone. Several travelers described the "Chunkey" game.
Courtesy of the Museum of Science and Natural History of the
Academy of Science of St. Louis

THE
DISCOVERIES
OF
JOHN LEDERER,

In three several Marches from

VIRGINIA,

To the West of

Carolina,

And other parts of the Continent:

Begun in *March* 1669, and ended in *September* 1670.

Together with

A General MAP of the whole Territory
which he traversed.

Collected and Translated out of Latine from his Discourse
and Writings,

By Sir *William Talbot* Baronet.

*Sed nos immensum spatiis confecimus aequor,
Et jam tempus equum fumantia solvere colla.* Virg. Georg.

London, Printed by *J. C.* for *Samuel Heyrick*, at Grays-
Inne-gate in Holborn. 1672.

Title Page of John Lederer, *The Discoveries of John Lederer, 1672.*
Courtesy of the Library of Congress

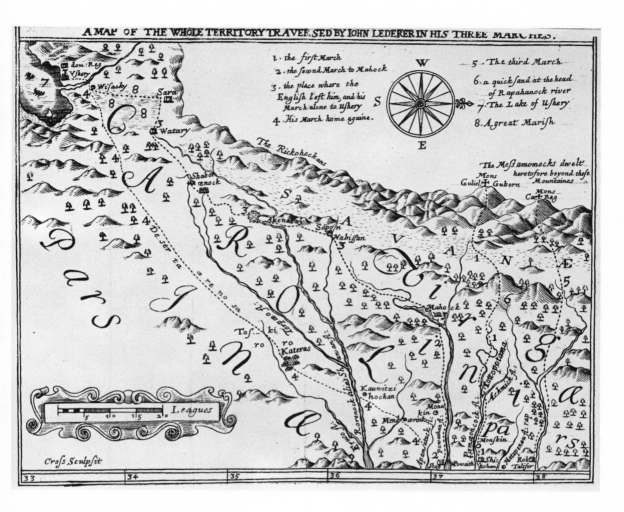

A Map of the Whole Territory Traversed by John Lederer in His Three Marches, 1672. The Lederer map was the basis for considerable cartographic misconception in the seventeenth century.
Courtesy of the Library of Congress

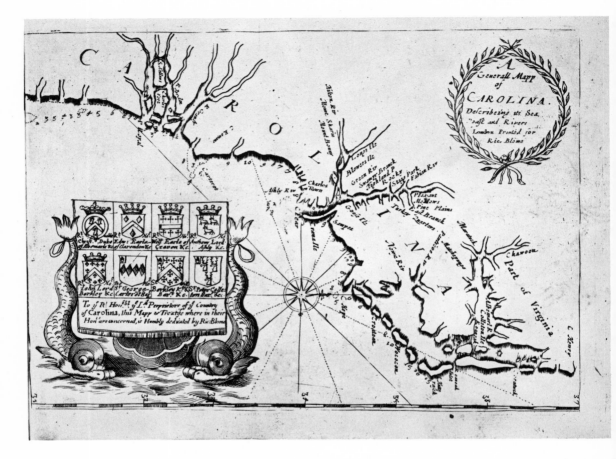

Richard Blome, *A Generall Mapp of Carolina*, 1672. Blome made use of information obtained by the Hilton and the Sandford expeditions.

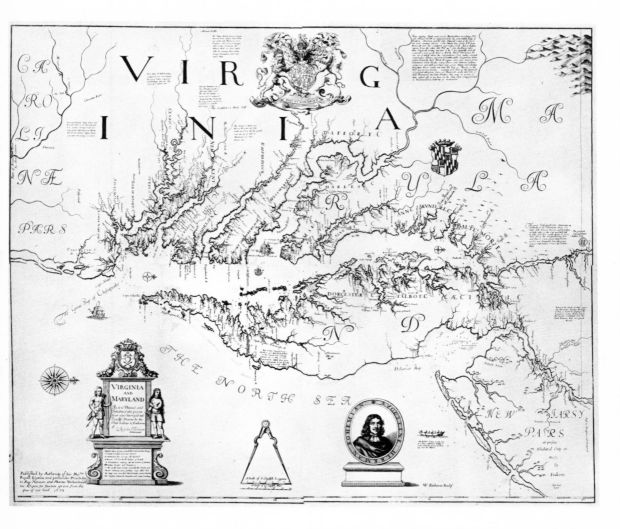

Augustin Herrman, *Virginia and Maryland*, 1673. One of the best maps of the second half of the
seventeenth century.
Courtesy of the Library of Congress

View here the Shadow whose Ingenious Hand
Hath drawne exact the Province Mary Land
Display'd her Glory in such Scænes of Witt
That those that read must fall in Love with it
For which his Labour hee deserves the praise
As well as Poets doe the wreath of Bays.

Anno Do: 1666. Ætatis Suæ 28.   H.W.

PHOTO-LITHOGR. CL. OSBORNE'S PROCESS

JS

A
CHARACTER
Of the PROVINCE of
MARY-LAND,

Wherein is Described in four distinct
Parts, (Viz.)

I. *The Scituation, and plenty of the Province.*
II. *The Laws, Customs, and natural Demea-
nor of the Inhabitant.*
III. *The worst and best Usage of a Mary-
Land Servant, opened in view.*
IV. *The Traffique, and vendable Commodities
of the Countrey.*

ALSO

A small *Treatise* on the wilde and
naked *INDIANS* (or *Susquehanokes*)
of *Mary-Land*, their Customs, Manners, Absurdities, & Religion.

Together with a Collection of Historical LETTERS.

By *GEORGE ALSOP*.

London, Printed by T. J. for *Peter Dring*,
at the sign of the Sun in the *Poultrey*: 1666.

Title Page of George Alsop, *A Character of the Province of Maryland*, 1666.

A NEW DESCRIPTION

OF THAT

Fertile and Pleasant Province

OF

CAROLINA:

WITH A

BRIEF ACCOUNT

OF ITS

Discovery, Settling,

AND THE

GOVERNMENT

Thereof to this Time.

With several Remarkable Passages of *Divine Providence* during my Time.

By *JOHN ARCHDALE:* Late *Governour of the same.*

LONDON:
Printed for *John Wyat,* at the *Rose* in St. *Paul's Church-Yard.* 1707.

Title Page of John Archdale, *A New Description of that Fertile and Pleasant Province of Carolina,* 1707.

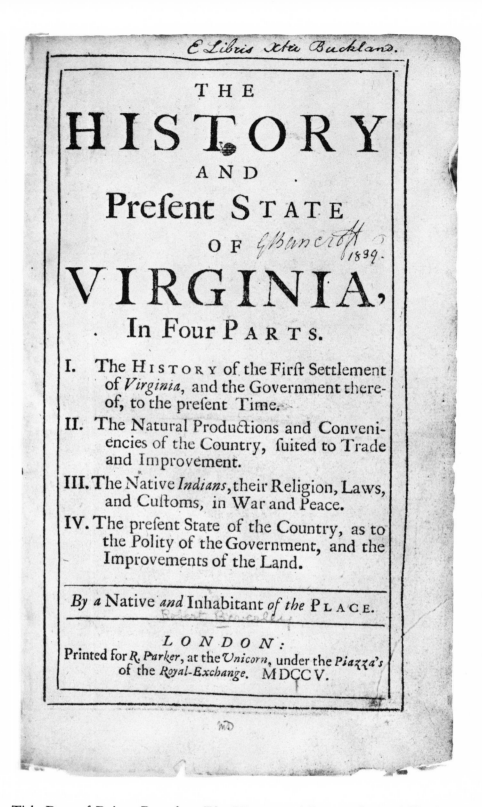

THE
HISTORY
AND
Present STATE
OF VIRGINIA,

In Four PARTS.

I. The HISTORY of the First Settlement of *Virginia*, and the Government thereof, to the present Time.

II. The Natural Productions and Conveniencies of the Country, suited to Trade and Improvement.

III. The Native *Indians*, their Religion, Laws, and Customs, in War and Peace.

IV. The present State of the Country, as to the Polity of the Government, and the Improvements of the Land.

By a Native *and* Inhabitant *of the* PLACE.

LONDON:
Printed for R. *Parker*, at the *Unicorn*, under the *Piazza's* of the *Royal-Exchange*. MDCCV.

Title Page of Robert Beverley, *The History and Present State of Virginia*, 1705.

THE
PRESENT STATE
OF
VIRGINIA.

GIVING

A particular and short Account of the *Indian*, *English*, and *Negroe* Inhabitants of that Colony.

Shewing their Religion, Manners, Government, Trade, Way of Living, *&c.* with a Description of the Country.

From whence is inferred a short VIEW of

MARYLAND *and* NORTH CAROLINA.

To which are added,

Schemes and Propositions for the better Promotion of Learning, Religion, Inventions, Manufactures, and Trade in *Virginia*, and the other *Plantations*.

For the Information of the *Curious*, and for the Service of such as are engaged in the *Propagation of the Gospel* and *Advancement of Learning*, and for the Use of all Persons concerned in the

Virginia *Trade and Plantation.*

GEN. ix. 27.

God shall enlarge JAPHETH, *and he shall dwell in the Tents of* SHEM, *and* CANAAN *shall be his Servant.*

By *HUGH JONES*, A. M. Chaplain to the Honourable Assembly, and lately Minister of *James-Town*, &c. in *Virginia*.

LONDON:
Printed for J. CLARKE, at the *Bible* under the *Royal-Exchange.* MDCCXXIV.

MD

Title Page of Hugh Jones, *The Present State of Virginia*, 1724.

How They Declare War. De Bry after Le Moyne. The De Bry engravings have been reproduced many times. Robert Beverley included several in his history of Virginia.

Hunting Deer. De Bry after Le Moyne. Several of the travelers commented on the use of animal skins for disguises and decoys.
Courtesy of the Smithsonian Institution National Anthropological Archives, Bureau of American Ethnology Collection

Mode of Drying Fish, Wild Animals, and Other Provisions. De Bry after Le Moyne.
Courtesy of the Smithsonian Institution National Anthropological Archives, Bureau of American Ethnology Collection

Preparations for a Feast. De Bry after Le Moyne.

Courtesy of the Smithsonian Institution National Anthropological Archives, Bureau of American Ethnology Collection

Ceremonies of Women Mourning for Their Deceased Husbands. De Bry after Le Moyne.

Courtesy of the Smithsonian Institution National Anthropological Archives, Bureau of American Ethnology Collection

Indians Making Canoes. De Bry after White.

Courtesy of the Smithsonian Institution National Anthropological Archives, Bureau of American Ethnology Collection

An Indian Idol. De Bry after White. Robert Beverley and John Lawson observed idols among the southeastern Indians.

he wrote a brief "narrative" of his journey. Although his chief pre-occupation was with products and natural history, he also made several remarks concerning the Indians. After praising the natives as hunters, he noted a religious ceremony used by the Indians to aid in locating game. The Englishman said that after an Indian was unsuccessful in killing a deer, he inscribed a picture of a squirrel on a tree and then "worshiped" the image. The hunter soon located another deer. The traveler noted also that Indians worshiped the heavenly bodies and believed in a supreme deity. His remarks concerning the Indians' fear of the Devil were similar to those of George Alsop; however, the eighteenth-century author believed that the Maryland Indians made annual, not quadrennial, human sacrifice.[28]

Like most Europeans who commented on the Southern Indians, the anonymous observer praised the physical appearance of the natives, but his descriptions of their dwellings differed from other accounts. The Indians he visited lived in watery areas and built their homes on stilts. Much of their diet consisted of oysters and fish. The Indians, however, practiced agriculture, with the women growing corn and melons. The unknown narrator's remarks concerning the life of the natives were brief, but he revealed more interest in them than did many of the travelers in the Southern colonies.[29]

During the last decades of the seventeenth century and the first of the eighteenth, Quakers often visited the English colonies in North America. Between 1671 and 1673, George Fox, founder of the Society of Friends, traveled through most of the colonies, including Maryland, Virginia, and North Carolina. The only Indians he noted in the South were the few who attended two Quaker meetings. On the first occasion his only comment was to point out that one of the men was a native "emperor" attended by several of his "kings." Later, with the aid of an interpreter, he preached to a small group of Indians led by an "emperor or governor." Except for the terse comments

---

[28] "Narrative of a Voyage to Maryland, 1705–1706," *American Historical Review*, Vol. XII (Jan., 1907), 327–40.

[29] *Ibid.*, 329–34.

expressing his opinion of the political organization of the red man, Fox made no observation on the Southern Indians.[30]

A quarter of a century later a prominent Quaker named Thomas Story landed in Virginia and during the next seven years visited all of the colonies from North Carolina northward. Story was interested in the native Americans but actually saw few of them. While visiting a Quaker in southern Virginia who had frequent contact with the Indians, he asked about their religion. Story learned that the Indians believed in reward and punishment after death and gained some idea of what these concepts meant to the Indian. "Hell" for these red men was a cold place whose inhabitants were always hungry, while "heaven" was warm, with plentiful food. Later, Story made his only visit to Southern Indians and enlarged his knowledge of Indian religion. In 1699 he made a one-day trip to a small Chickahominy village on the Mattapony River in Virginia. At first the natives, members of the Powhatan tribal family, were suspicious of his desire to assemble them, but Story soon convinced them of his peaceful intentions and preached to them. Afterwards, he questioned the chief or "Sagamor" about his theology. The Quaker was pleased to learn that the Indian leader believed in a soul which lived after the death of the earthly body. The Englishman may have been gratified to learn of this Christian concept from a heathen, but he believed nevertheless that the Europeans had greatly harmed the Indians. Story accused whites of teaching Indians drunkenness, stealing, lying, and prostitution, in addition to cheating them.[31]

As brief as Story's comments were regarding the Indian, they were more detailed than those by other Quakers. In 1698, Thomas Chalkley visited some Indians in Maryland, and his sole remark was that "they were kind to us."[32] Two decades later, John Farmer preached to some Quakers and about thirty Indians in Maryland but

[30] George Fox, *Journal or Historical Account of the Life, Travels, Suffering, Christian Experiences and Labour of Love of . . . George Fox,* 499–500, 519.

[31] Thomas Story, *Journal of the Life of Thomas Story,* 156, 162–63.

[32] Thomas Chalkley, *Journal or Historical Account of the Life, Travels, and Christian Experiences of . . . Thomas Chalkley,* 14.

made no comment on the Indians or their reaction to his words.[33] Other Quakers who visited the colonies in the seventeenth and eighteenth centuries, including Samuel Bownas, John Griffith, Benjamin Holme, and William Edmundson, traveled widely but either avoided Southern Indians or did not record their observations.[34]

In several accounts of travel in Maryland, Virginia, and the Carolinas in the second half of the seventeenth century and the first decades of the eighteenth, the authors revealed an interest in the Southern Indians. Yet the writing of the early colonizers and officials of the Carolinas, of the missionaries of the Venerable Society, and of the various men who dealt with Maryland and Virginia indicated that they were more interested in making known the strange, savage customs of the Indians than in understanding them. The comments were usually brief, and the observations dealt almost entirely with the obvious manifestations of native culture and society. Beginning in the early eighteenth century, another group of writers was showing considerably more interest and sympathy for the natives of America.

[33] [John Farmer], "First American Journey, 1711–1714," ed. H. J. Cadbury, American Antiquarian Soc., *Proceedings*, n. s., LIII, 86.

[34] Samuel Bownas, *Account of the Life, Travels, and Christian Experiences in the Work of the Ministry of Samuel Bownas*, ed. J. Besse; John Griffith, *Journal of the Life, Travels, and Labours in the Work of the Ministry of John Griffith*; Benjamin Holme, *Collection of the Epistles and Works*; and William Edmundson, *Journal of the Life, Travels, Suffering, and Labour of Love in the Work of . . . William Edmundson.*

IV

Impressions of the Virginia Indians:
Beverley and Jones

URING the first decades of the eighteenth century, some Englishmen in the Southern colonies demonstrated an awakened interest in the American Indian. Although there were still examples of the earlier type of observations of the strange native customs, several of the colonists wrote accounts which indicated their acceptance of the Indian as another human being rather than as some exotic creature who might be discussed but not understood. Five of these writers, Robert Beverley II, Hugh Jones, William Byrd II, and John and Peter Fontaine, limited their comments to the Indians of Virginia; three of them shared a belief in intermarriage as the solution to conflict between the white and red races. Only one of them, Hugh Jones, revealed a highly critical attitude toward the natives.

Robert Beverley II, the second son of a Virginia aristocrat, had all the advantages that wealth and family prestige could offer. His English ancestors were minor gentry of Yorkshire, but his father became one of the most prominent men in seventeenth-century Virginia. Major Robert Beverley went to the Old Dominion in 1663 and soon emerged as one of the colony's political leaders. During Bacon's Rebellion, Major Beverley was among Governor William Berkeley's most zealous supporters. Indeed, he continued to support the royal governor even after his recall, consistently opposing subsequent governors and their colonial adherents. The elder Beverley also incurred the animosity of some of his neighbors when he took part in a movement to reduce the colony's tobacco surplus. In 1682 tobacco prices fell disastrously, and Major Beverley and a few other planters sought to improve prices by destroying part of their neighbors' tobacco crop. For that act he was later forced to seek pardon on bended knee before the Council, but the submission, distasteful as it was, did not seem to humble the fiery old man. In addition to his interest in politics, Major Beverley found the time and means to acquire a large estate, and at his death in 1687 he left some fifty thousand acres of land and £5,000 of personal property to his heirs.

Robert Beverley II, whose character was similar to his father's, was educated in England, and upon his return to the New World he quickly secured minor positions in the Virginia government. In 1698 young Beverley enhanced his social position by marrying Ursula Byrd, the daughter of William Byrd I, who because of his wealth and membership on the Council surpassed even the elder Beverley in prominence. Beverley found it necessary to return to England in 1703 to protect his interests in a case before the Privy Council. In London he became incensed at some disparaging remarks by Governor Francis Nicholson and Surveyor-General of the Customs Robert Quarry regarding Virginia and her political leaders. In some letters and in a published work, young Beverley made equally indiscreet comments about those officials as well as some of his countrymen. His imprudence ended his chances for political advancement, and thereafter Beverley was not on a friendly basis with many of his fellow aristocrats. After his return to America, he retired to his Beverley Park estate and lived a comfortable but thrifty life.[1]

The publication which contained the unfavorable reflections was *The History and Present State of Virginia*, printed in London in 1705. Beverley wrote his account to correct the errors of another eighteenth-century author. While in London, the Virginian had been

[1] Wright, *First Gentlemen of Virginia*, Chap. x; and Beverley, *History and Present State of Virginia*, ed. Louis B. Wright, preface and introduction.

asked to read and offer suggestions on a manuscript portion of *The British Empire in America* by John Oldmixon. Despite Oldmixon's heavy reliance upon information obtained from William Byrd II, Beverley found Oldmixon or his brother-in-law so much in error that he believed correction impossible. Instead, he decided to write his own history. Beverley divided his writing into four parts. The first dealt with the history of the colony, the second with the natural history of Virginia, the third with the Indians, and the fourth with the colony's government.

In 1722 a revised edition of the work was published, and it contained some significant changes. For Beverley's contemporaries the most important difference probably was the deletion and modification of the indiscreet characterizations of prominent Virginians. In the Preface, he explained the changes by stating that he had discussed the government of the colony "without reflection upon the private conduct of any person."[2] Evidently the more mature Beverley was not so ready to reveal his political prejudices and opinions to the world. The reason for two other modifications was not as apparent. In the 1705 edition of his book, Beverley highly praised the beauty and innocence of the Indian women and strongly urged intermarriage between whites and Indians as a means of improving racial relations.[3] Seventeen years later the proposal for miscegenation was deleted and the praise of women was modified. Beverley gave no reason for these revisions, but the changes might have been due to his conclusion that successful intermarriage was not possible or practical on a large scale. In 1717 Alexander Spotswood, lieutenant-governor of Virginia, stated his belief that intermarriage was not the answer to white-Indian problems because, despite years of contact on the frontier, he could not find even one marriage between the two races. He apparently approved of the possibility and certainly did not condemn it.[4] Beverley may have been

[2] Preface to the 1722 edition.

[3] Beverley, *History and Present State of Virginia*, 38–39, 170–71.

[4] *Official Letters of Alexander Spotswood, Lieutenant-Governor of the Colony of Virginia, 1710–1722*, ed. R. A. Brock, II, 227.

disillusioned by the deterioration in relations between the English and the Southern Indians. The Southern colonies suffered directly or indirectly from the Tuscarora War of 1711–1713 and the Yamassee War of 1715–1716, but while Robert Beverley must have known of these events, he did not consider them important enough to add to the 1722 edition of his history.[5]

Beverley sought to discuss intelligently his homeland and its products, government, and inhabitants. To supplement his personal knowledge, he used the writings of such men as Captain John Smith, Thomas Hariot, and Samuel Purchas. His desire to comment honestly upon the natives of Virginia was apparent in the statement that the Indian material in his work was "a true Account of the *Indians* . . . by my own Knowledge or by credible Information." His interest went beyond the mere observation of the natives; Beverley tried to understand fully the red man. On one occasion he visited a village and found the Indians reluctant to discuss their religion. Indeed, the Englishman learned that whites were forbidden to visit the Indians' "House of Religious Worship." But Beverley found the opportunity to visit the place in the absence of the natives. Another time, he plied an Indian guest with liquor to learn about the native religion.

For secondary works on the Southern Indians, the Virginian seemed to favor the writings of Captain Smith, but he also revealed an acquaintance with other writers. In a discussion of the language of the Virginia Indians, Beverley admitted his uncertainty about the connection between the language of the Southern natives and the "Algonkine" discussed by Louis A., Baron de Lahontan. Finally, it should be noted that although Beverley desired accuracy, he did not indicate by names the Indian tribes or groups whose culture he described.[6]

[5] Wright feels that Beverley's defense of Indian virtues and the suggestion about miscegenation were highly unusual for an eighteenth-century Englishman. *First Gentlemen of Virginia*, 309. If this were true, one might conclude that the 1722 revisions were made to appease contemporary opinion; however, as will be seen in this study, most of the observers of the Southern Indians praised the virtues of the Indians, and at least three other men proposed intermarriage as a means of improving white-Indian relations.

[6] Beverley, *History and Present State of Virginia*, 11, 191–204.

Beverley began his discussion of the native Americans with several pages of comments about their diet and their methods of securing the food. He briefly noted several foodstuffs, including four types of corn and a wild "Sugar-Tree." He paid more attention to hunting methods. Fish were caught by traps as well as by gigging and grappling. Fowl were taken with bow and arrow. For large game such as "Elks, Buffaloes, Deer," fires were sometimes set to encircle the animals and force them into the center where they were killed. The manner of food preparation hardly interested Beverley, but he did mention a "Homony" made of fish being cooked over an open fire. He compared the food and its preparation to practices of the ancient Spartans. Perhaps because the Indians' table manners were so different from those of Europeans, he observed that the red man sat on the ground while eating, the container of food placed between his outstretched legs.[7]

Beverley also commented upon the appearance of the Indians and their dwellings. He praised the physiques of the natives and stated that he had never heard of a misshapen Indian. Both sexes removed facial and body hair with "Muscle-shell" tweezers, and both wore a "mantle" of cloth or skins around their waist and buckskin moccasins. The "common sort" of men wore only a breechcloth. Beverley noted that women wore ornaments of *"Conque* shell," but he wrote little about men's decorations. The Indians lived in villages of between fifty and five hundred families. Some of the villages were surrounded by ten or twelve-foot palisades, but in others only the "King's House" was protected by walls. Beverley described two house patterns. Dwellings, or "Wigwangs," were either oblong or shaped like a "Bee-hive" with a smoke hole in the top. He also commented on the division of villagers into family units during the hunting season.[8]

The Virginian's attention to the religion of his dark-skinned contemporaries was apparent; he devoted more pages to the topic than to any other aspect of native culture. Beverley viewed religious leaders

[7] *Ibid.*, 136–45.
[8] *Ibid.*, 156–66, 174–77.

of any sort with distaste. He believed that "Priests" exercised too great a control over the people of all nations. Beverley not only pointed out that native "Priests," who were "hideously ugly," had a distinctive hair style and dress, but he quoted Captain Smith to some length on the subject of medicine men and Indian sacrifice practices. He questioned Smith's veracity regarding human sacrifice and noted offerings of tobacco and other things such as part of war booty or a successful hunt. When he dared to enter the forbidden "House of Worship," he opened some sacred mats and found old bones, tomahawks, and images which were called "Okee," "Quioccos," or "Kiwasa" by the various tribes. The Englishman also saw and described the "Huskanawing," a boys' puberty ritual. He believed that the youths were given a drug that caused them to forget their boyhood ways. He first believed that the purpose of the rite was to permit the older men to obtain the "wealth" of the boys, but he finally concluded that the "Huskanawing" was an initiation into manhood.[9]

The History and Present State of Virginia also contained brief comments on other aspects of the Indians' religion. When Beverley loosened the tongue of an Indian visitor with alcohol, the native revealed that he believed in a god "in the Heavens above" and in evil spirits which had to be appeased. Beverley related a story of an Indian bringing rain to the plantation of his father-in-law, "Collonel Byrd." He also reported that a rock on Byrd's land was sacred to the red men because it contained the impressions of "giant footprints." Toward the end of his comments on native religion, the Virginian noted that the Indians erected "altars" to commemorate special events.[10]

Robert Beverley made shorter comments on other aspects of Indian civilization. He believed that the natives were governed by "Kings." Some of the monarchs ruled more than one "Town" or "Kingdom," and in this case, a "Viceregent" acted as the "King's" representative. Seemingly, the most important responsibility of the "Viceregent" was the collection of tribute to be paid his superior. The

9 *Ibid.*, 164–66, 201–12.
10 *Ibid.*, 200–201, 204–205, 211, 213.

privileged status of the rulers continued after death. Bones were re-moved from the corpses of "Kings and Rulers" and replaced with sand. The body was then preserved with oil and placed in a special house. Most of Beverley's comments regarding war dealt with the common customs of holding a council, arousing emotions by dances, and using war paints, as well as the lack of discrimination as to age or sex in warfare. He noted that the Indians sometimes actually buried a *"Tomahawk"* following successful peace negotiations. Beverley did not mention the smoking of a peace pipe between former enemies, but he did report that foes would not smoke together and quoted Father Louis Hennepin on this custom.[11]

Regarding the social mores of the red men, Beverley was especially interested in the status of women. He observed that "Strangers of Condition" were given two "young Beautiful Virgins," but he quickly pointed out that the brief encounters did not hurt the girls' reputation. Indeed, he thought that the ancients of the European world might have had similar customs. He felt that such unchastity was uncommon and stated his disbelief in stories of Indian prostitution, commenting that for an unwed woman to have a child was a barrier to marriage. Although divorce was easy, Beverley reported that spouses were faithful while together. His remarks regarding the matrilineal descent of the Virginia tribes were interesting. Without explanation, he attributed the method of descent to a basic "Jealousy" on the part of the natives. The reason for the inclusion of the comment in a section entitled *"Of the War, and Peace of the Indians"* was also not apparent.[12]

The arts and crafts of the Indians also received Beverley's attention. He reported that each village had a sweat house and that sweating, scratching with "Rattle-Snakes Tooth," localized searing, and herbal medicines were the common means of curing illness. The

---

[11] *Ibid.*, 174, 186–88, 192–94.

[12] *Ibid.*, 170, 189, 193. Beverley was mistaken about the chastity of the women. Driver notes that premarital sex and prostitution were common in the Southeast and that there was very little if any stigma attached to premarital pregnancy. *Indians of North America*, 267.

Indians' use of pictographs was noted, but no details were provided. Beverley did devote two pages to a discussion of "Peak" and the less valued "Roenoke," which were used as media of exchange. Although he included in his work a long quotation from Captain Smith on the dances of the Indians, he had a low opinion of native music and dancing. Toward the end of his narration, Beverley commented on the manufacturing of the native Americans. Despite the Indians' apparent limitations in using only fire and "scrapers" to hollow out a tree, he indicated that he had seen canoes up to thirty feet in length. He also noted that the Indians used a variety of native products in making other items. He mentioned bows of locust wood, arrows of reeds, glue from deer horns, baskets of "Silk grass," and earthen pottery.[13]

Like most of his contemporaries, Beverley commented on the effect of European civilization on the Indian. In discussing the political system of the natives, he noted that they had generally adopted English titles for their officials. He was more concerned, however, with the adverse effects of white contact. Living in a "simple State of Nature," Beverley said, the Indians

have on several accounts reasons to lament the arrival of the Europeans, by whose means they seem to have lost their Felicity, as well as their Innocence. The *English* have taken away great part of their Country, and consequently made everything less plenty amongst them. They have introduced Drunkenness and Luxury amongst them, which have multiply'd their Wants, and put them upon desiring a thousand things, they never dreamt of before.[14]

Robert Beverley generally succeeded in giving an honest account of the Virginia Indians as he knew them. Whenever his own knowledge or conclusions indicated that other writers had erred, as Captain John Smith did in his account of human sacrifice, Beverley presented his own opinion. He included in his work fourteen engravings made more than a hundred years before and which dealt with Indians other than those he observed, but his descriptions were not too

[13] Beverley, *History and Present State of Virginia*, 190, 217–24, 229–30.
[14] *Ibid.*, 226, 233.

dissimilar from them. In the preface to his book, Beverley said "I am an Indian, and don't pretend to be exact in my language."[15] The cultivated gentleman of Beverley Park was not, of course, "an Indian," but the remark aptly revealed his sympathy for the native Americans.

The Reverend Mr. Hugh Jones, a contemporary of Beverley's and author of another history of Virginia, did not share that sympathy. Jones, probably an Oxford graduate, came to Virginia in 1716 and quickly became a part of the colony's public life. He taught mathematics at William and Mary College, served as chaplain of the House of Burgesses, and ministered to congregations at Jamestown and Williamsburg. After five years he returned to England, and in 1724 his *The Present State of Virginia* was published in London.[16]

The book has been praised as one of the better accounts of early eighteenth-century Virginia,[17] but the twenty pages devoted to Indians were not as perceptive as the remainder of the work. In his attempt to describe the Indian, Jones exhibited several handicaps. The English minister's personal knowledge of the American Indian was limited, and he indicated that most of his information came from the Reverend Mr. Charles Griffin, who taught the Saponi and other

[15] The author's reason for the statement is not readily apparent, but Moses C. Tyler probably came close to the truth when he wrote: "He [Beverley] identified himself with them [Indians] by playfully calling himself an Indian . . . ." *History of American Literature, 1607–1765*, 493. It should be noted that the author's characterization of the writing of Beverley differs in emphasis from that of Harvey Pearce. Pearce feels that Beverley was more concerned with portraying the Indians as latter-day "Spartans" than in presenting an accurate picture of their culture. He cites three examples to support his thesis: the comparisons between Indian food and that of the Spartans, the giving of companions for the night by the Indians and Beverley's suspicion that this may have happened in the ancient world, and the "Spartan-like" appearance of the engravings. *Savages of America*, 42–43. Actually, the Virginia author made few comparisons with the ancients, and viewers may well disagree on the impression conveyed by the engravings. It might also be noted that Pearce incorrectly gives the title of Beverley's book as *History of the Present State of Virginia. Ibid.*, 42.

[16] The identity of the "Hugh Jones" who wrote the history of Virginia has been a subject of controversy. See Nelson Rightmyer, "Hugh Jones, Colonial Enigma," *Maryland Historical Magazine*, Vol. XLVII (Sept., 1952), 263–64 and (Dec., 1952), 354–55; and Richard L. Morton, "The Reverend Hugh Jones, Lord Baltimore's Mathematician," *William and Mary Quarterly*, 3rd ser., Vol. VII (Jan., 1950), 107–15.

[17] Clark, *Travels in the Old South*, I, 95.

tributary Indians at Fort Christanna, near present Gholsonville, Virginia. That some of his account was based on personal observation was apparent from his remarks and his comment that, in addition to material furnished by Griffin, he included "such as I have seen and known myself."[18]

Other liabilities that influenced the minister's understanding of the red man were his beliefs about the origin of the natives and his stronger sentiments regarding Indian morality. After a brief warning about the difficulty of determining the "Pedigree" of the "Aborigines," Jones devoted five pages to the topic. He believed that Europeans and some Asians were descendants of the youngest son of Noah; Egyptians, Moors, and Negroes had descended from the middle son; and Hebrews and the Indians originated with Shem, the eldest son. He cited Genesis 10:25–32 and a similarity between Hebrew and Indian customs to support his assertions. Yet, the only instance in which Jones noted a parallel concerned the division of both groups into tribes and families dominated by patriarchs. He also conjectured that the red men had arrived in America from eastern Asia. In his opinion, the migration might have begun because a boat of Indians was driven across the ocean by a storm or perhaps because America and Asia had once been joined. He was certain, however, that they had not come from Africa, because the African custom of circumcision was not found among the American Indians.[19]

Although he stated that the "Aborigines" were not totally lacking in praiseworthy attributes, Jones's attitude toward Indians was one of distrust and condemnation. His brief comment on warfare centered upon the treatment of prisoners who were killed by scalping or burned with "scewers of Light wood which burn like Torches." He condemned the natives for permitting cows given them to die because of inattention. He believed that an Indian "Priest or Physician" used chants "only to blind the common Indian." Finally, to the Englishman the Virginia Indians were usually

[18] Jones, *Present State of Virginia*, 8, 15.
[19] *Ibid.*, 2–7.

treacherous, suspicious and jealous, difficult to be persuaded or imposed upon, and very sharp, hard in Dealing, and ingenious in their Way, and in Things that they naturally know or have been taught, though at first they are very obstinate, and unwilling to apprehend or learn Novelties, and seem stupid and silly to Strangers.

The only exceptions to this harsh characterization were a few "great Men" or leaders—all unidentified—who were honest and just. Ingenious Indian traits included the knowledge of the geography of their habitat, their ability to compute time by the sun, moon, and the annual flights of "Cohonks, a sort of wild Geese," and some artistic ability.[20]

Despite their imperfections, Jones believed that the native Americans were capable and worthy of being Christianized. He blamed the failure of missionary efforts on inadequate knowledge, saying that missionaries "rarely see an Indian." They remained among the Europeans instead. He indicated that some Indians were willing to have their children educated by whites but did not want the children's attitudes changed because "they [the Indians] did not desire us [the English] to turn Indian." Jones was one of the very few whites to report resistance on such a logical basis. The author neither commented upon the attitude nor seemed to feel that it might be important to the missionary effort.[21]

Jones's other comments regarding the Virginia natives dealt mainly with their culture. In discussing the appearance of the Indians, he suggested that the custom of strapping the young native baby to a cradle board resulted in erect posture and commented that it was extremely rare to see a deformed Indian. Body decorations by painting and tattooing and the distinctive hair styles of each "Nation" were also noted. Jones also indirectly indicated that acculturation was taking place among the Indians. He stated that although red men often wore clothing made of deer skins, they liked brightly colored European

[20] *Ibid.*, 8–17. Beverley indicated that "Cohonks" meant "winters" and that the Indians took the name from the sound made by wild geese. *History and Present State of Virginia,* 211.

[21] Jones, *Present State of Virginia,* 1, 15, 18.

cloth. Only the boys used bows and arrows; the men preferred and seemed to have firearms. Villages were "meanly defended with Pales" and contained a "Forum" or open area in the center for public meetings. Jones apparently had a higher opinion of the women than of the men, for he indicated that

the Women do all the hard Labour, such as cutting down the Trees, planting Corn, Etc. carrying Burthens [*sic*] and all their other Work; the Men only hunting, fishing and fowling, eating, drinking and sleeping.[22]

It was apparent that Jones did not conceive of the Indian man's economic contributions as equal to that of the woman.

The comments of the English minister concerning religion and social customs were only slightly more detailed. He witnessed a burial at Fort Christanna and later described the ceremony. The corpse was dressed "in the best Cloth they could buy with the Skins of the Deceased" and buried with "Cloth, Skins and Nicknacks." There was much "howling Lamentations and Purgation." The natives, according to Jones, believed that the dead went to "Mohomny" which was "beyond the Sun" and there had plenty of food. If they had been evil, they went to a place inhabited by dangerous animals and having little food. Jones noted that polygamy was permitted if a man could maintain more than one wife. An adulterous woman's hair was cut, and she was forced into exile or slavery or put to death. The Indian portion of *The Present State of Virginia* concluded with an appeal for greater missionary effort, but the author sadly commented that such attempts were hampered by the Indians' disillusionment with Christianity because so many whites were "debauched."[23]

Hugh Jones later returned to America and served various parishes in Maryland until his death in 1760. Evidently the 1724 publication was his only work to deal with the American Indians. His attitude towards the red man was somewhat ambivalent. While he urged that greater efforts be made to Christianize them, he charac-

[22] *Ibid.*, 9–11.
[23] *Ibid.*, 16, 18–20.

terized them as "difficult, obstinate, and unwilling to apprehend or learn Novelties." Perhaps for Jones the difficulties only made the glories of missionary work greater, but he never chose to undertake the task.

Robert Beverley II and Hugh Jones revealed very different impressions of the natives of Virginia. Jones's knowledge of the Indians was limited. He was suspicious of the natives' intentions and questioned their intelligence. Beverley's interest was more profound. His acquaintance with several books about red men and his brief but frequent contacts with them increase the validity of his *History*. Beverley was sympathetic to the plight of the Indians and quickly defended them against charges of immorality.

V

Impressions of the Virginia Indians:
Byrd and the Fontaines

THREE other Virginians of the early eighteenth century recorded their impressions of Indian civilization. William Byrd II, Robert Beverley's brother-in-law, personally observed Indians several times during his life and often recorded his reactions in his various writings. John and Peter Fontaine, immigrants to the colony, had less contact with the natives and left few comments of their observations. None of the men wrote formal histories, but Byrd and John Fontaine revealed an interest in the red man and some understanding of his culture.

William Byrd II was one of the most cultured and educated men of colonial Virginia. His father had acquired wealth and considerable social and political importance in the colony, though he was of middle-class origin in the Old World. William Byrd II was educated in England where he not only attended the Middle Temple and was admitted to the bar but also gained a broader knowledge of the world through travel, regular attendance at the theatres, a short period of service with a business firm, and membership in the Royal Society. Upon his return to Virginia in 1696 he was elected to the House of Burgesses, and in 1697 he returned to London to act as the colony's agent. In 1704 the elder Byrd died and the son went home to claim his inheritance. By 1708 he had become a member of the Council, a position he held until his death in 1744. He also secured other governmental offices during his lifetime, serving once as head of the Virginia commission which, with a North Carolina counterpart, surveyed more than one hundred miles of the two colonies' boundary in 1728.

From his experiences as a boundary commissioner Byrd wrote the *History of the Dividing Line*, which he intended for publication. Despite several revisions, he was never satisfied with the work, and it remained in manuscript for nearly a century after his death. He also wrote a more candid account of the journey, *Secret History of the Dividing Line*, for the amusement of his friends. This work and three diaries which Byrd kept were not published until the twentieth century.[1]

In his writings William Byrd II, unlike Beverley, did not attempt to deal comprehensively with the Virginia Indians. Indeed, he recorded in his diary several visits to his home by native Americans without making any comment that revealed his impression or attitude toward them.[2] He did record in his diary some observations of the red men. In October, 1711, Byrd visited an Indian village and noted the entertainment provided by his hosts. The boys held an archery contest, and the girls ran foot races. The men contributed to the festivities with a war dance, and a "love dance" was performed by the women.[3]

The best indications of Byrd's opinion of the Indians were contained in the two *Histories*. The party of Virginia commissioners that participated in surveying the boundary line included a Saponi Indian guide and hunter named Ned Bearskin. Byrd evidently was fond of the Indian and often sought out his company. Indian religion

---

[1] For discussions of the two *Histories*, see Wright, *First Gentlemen of Virginia*, 336–37; and William Byrd, *Histories of the Dividing Line betwixt Virginia and North Carolina*, ed. William K. Boyd, xvi. The diaries are *Secret Diary of William Byrd of Westover, 1709–1712*, ed. Louis B. Wright and Marion Tinling; *Another Secret Diary of William Byrd of Westover, 1739–1741*, ed. Maude H. Woodfin and Marion Tinling; and *London Diary (1717–1721) and Other Writings*, ed. Louis B. Wright and Marion Tinling. In this study, the writer has used William Byrd, *Prose Works, Narratives of a Colonial Virginian*, ed. Louis B. Wright.

[2] For example, see Byrd, *London Diary*, 390, 410, 503–504, 510, 512, 518.

[3] Byrd, *Secret Diary, 1709–1712*, 724–25.

interested Byrd, and he questioned the guide at length. The English-man learned that Bearskin had a concept of a "supreme god" and an even more vivid concept of afterlife. According to the guide, both the "good" and the "bad" traveled down the same "road" after death. They were soon separated by a bolt of lightning, and the "good" went to a place where they always remained young, where it was always warm, and where there was always enough food. The opposite awaited the "bad." The Indian conceived of "hell" as a place of continual cold, hunger, and pain. The ruler of the terrible place was "a dreadful old woman . . . whose head is covered with rattlesnakes instead of tresses, with glaring white eyes that strike a terror unspeakable into all that behold her." Bearskin did believe that the "miserable wretches" con-signed to this place received another chance. After a period of time dependent upon the seriousness of their guilt, they were returned to earth to see if they would "mend their manners and merit a place the next time in the regions of bliss."[4]

Byrd noted a myth concerning the Tuscarora Indians. After reporting the tribe's decline and its disastrous war with North Caro-lina, after which most of the survivors fled north, he stated that the natives believed their troubles were the result of a god's vengeance. A "messenger from Heaven" had been sent to warn the Tuscaroras of their wicked and evil ways, but instead of paying heed, the Indians killed him. For the act, the god began punishing the Tuscaroras. He would not cease "till he shall have blotted every living soul of them out of the world."

Byrd learned from Bearskin the importance that the Indians attached to the observation of certain taboos. The guide was upset to discover that Europeans cooked turkey and venison in the same pot. He warned his employers to stop the practice before the "Spirit" frightened away all the game. A few days later the Indian refused to bring a turkey he had killed into camp because the English persisted in mixing "the Beasts of the Fields and the Beasts of the Air." On this occasion, Byrd noted the similarity between "Indian Superstition" and

[4] Byrd, *Prose Works*, 118–20, 246–48.

the "Levitical Law, which forbade the mixing of things of a Different Nature together in the same field, or in the Same Garment, and [he added] why not then in the same Kettle?" Byrd evidently was impressed with this belief because several years later he made another comment on the superstition.[5]

In his *History*, Byrd indicated less serious aspects of his knowledge of the Indian. He was not the only commissioner interested in them and their beliefs. One evening Byrd overheard another of the whites talking with Ned Bearskin. A thunderstorm was in progress at the time, and the Indian asked the Englishman to explain the thunder. The man replied that an English god was shooting at an Indian god and that the lightning was the flash of the gun. According to Byrd, Bearskin, "carrying on the Humor replied very gravely," that it must be true and that the rain must result from "the Indian god's being so scared he could not hold his water." On another occasion a member of the party killed a squirrel, and the "merry Indian" told of the unusual manner in which these animals crossed water. The squirrel was supposed to sit on a small piece of wood and, by using his tail as a sail, be pushed across by the wind. Elsewhere, Byrd reported that he had learned of the Indian custom of capturing alligators by mounting the reptile and quickly placing a length of wood between the beast's jaws. Unable to close its mouth, the alligator could not submerge and eventually grew so weary that the Indian was able to kill and eat him. Byrd also included a similar story of an Occaneechi Indian who captured a very large sturgeon by slipping a noose over the sleeping fish.[6]

The commissioner gained firsthand information about the Indian method of curing deerskins. Each evening the Indian guide preserved the skins of the deer killed that day. Byrd seemed to admire the simplicity of the technique, which consisted of rubbing the animal's brains on the hide and then smoking it, but he did not like the strong

[5] *Ibid.*, 101, 116–18, 231, 239, 243–44, 302–304, 390.

[6] *Ibid.*, 307, 310, 316–17. Regarding the capture of the alligator, Wright notes that Pliny related a story of the people of the Nile capturing crocodiles by the same method. *Ibid.*, 310n.

odor produced by the drying. He emphasized the importance of such skins as an item of trade, devoting several pages to the value of the white-Indian trade and discussing the famous Trading Path that ran through the Virginia and Carolina Piedmont.

Byrd had a high regard for the Indian belief in the value of bear meat as a cure for sterility. Under questioning, Bearskin somewhat reluctantly reported that Indian women were seldom childless because a husband who desired children would eat bear meat for six weeks; almost always the wife would have a child in nine months. Indeed, Byrd's conviction of the Indian's truthfulness was strengthened by his knowledge that every member of the boundary party except for the Reverend Mr. Fontaine was a proud father some nine months after their return home.[7]

The Virginia aristocrat was generally appreciative of the Indian and his culture, but occasionally he became critical. In his discussion of native hunting methods, Byrd condemned the "unmerciful Sport [which] is called Fire Hunting." The natives would set fire to the woods in a large circle, and the Englishman deplored the resulting death of animal and plant life within the circle. He softened his criticism by noting that the ancient Persians' ring of men was somewhat similar. Byrd also disliked the Indian method of warfare with its ambushes, scalping, and torture, but again he noted a similar practice among some ancient people. Indeed, for him the fact that both the American Indians and the ancient Scythians scalped their slain enemies was "not the least proof of their [the Indians'] Original [origin?] from the Northern Inhabitants of Asia."[8] The methods of hunting and warfare were among the very few aspects of native culture that Byrd openly criticized.

On two occasions during the surveying expedition, Byrd came into contact with Indians other than the guide Ned Bearskin. In April, 1728, the commissioners decided to suspend their work until autumn because of the increasing danger from rattlesnakes, which were becom-

---

[7] *Ibid.*, 230, 232, 274–75, 278, 292–93, 307–11.
[8] *Ibid.*, 258–60, 299–300, 313.

ing more active as the weather grew warmer. On their way home, they spent a day visiting a Nottoway Indian village near the Nottoway River in southeastern Virginia. In November, 1728, on their return journey following the completion of the survey, the commissioners were met by a group of Saponi Indians and invited to visit their village at Fort Christanna. Although the whites declined the invitation in November because of their desire to hasten home, Byrd recorded both encounters in his *Histories*.

Byrd's remarks concerning the Nottoway Indians, part of the Tuscarora tribal family, were more detailed than any of his other observations on the native Americans. He noted that the village of some two hundred people was about three hundred feet square and enclosed by a ten foot wall that extended slightly outward at the top to make assault more difficult. The houses were "no other but close arbors made of saplings, arched at the top and covered so well with bark as to be proof against all weather." The dwellings were warmed by a fire in the center, but there were no smoke holes in the roofs. The furnishings consisted of "hurdles" covered with mats and skins.[9]

The appearance of the natives drew Byrd's attention. The men had painted their bodies and performed "sundry war dances" being accompanied by a drum, "that is, a large gourd with a skin braced taut over the mouth of it." The women had also prepared for the visit and "were wrapped in their red and blue matchcoats, thrown so negligently about them that their mahogany skins appeared in several parts." The women also wore all of their "peak," which Byrd noted served as both money and jewelry. The Englishman was impressed by the women's erect posture but was repulsed by their coating of dirt and bear's oil. Despite the filth of the women, in the *Secret History* Byrd candidly reported that several of the party, even some of the commissioners, sought out the women. The arrangements were privately made, for the author complained that the party was so large that the red men were unable to furnish "bedfellows" for everyone as was their custom. The difference between the *History* and the *Secret History* is clearly

[9] *Ibid.*, 81, 217–19.

shown in this incident. In the *History* he wrote that "we were un-luckily so many that they could not well make us the compliments of bedfellows according to the Indian rules of hospitality, though a grave matron whispered one of the commissioners very civilly in the ear that if her daughter had been but one year older she should have been at his devotion." In the *Secret History* he recorded that "they offered us no bedfellows, according to the good Indian fashion, which we had reason to take unkindly. Only the Queen of Weyanoke told Steddy [Byrd] that her daughter had been at his service if she had not been too young."[10]

Although Byrd did criticize the "ladies that game" or en-gaged in prostitution for being "a little mercenary in their amours," he believed that such activities increased rather than hurt the women's reputations in the opinion of the Indians. The interest of William Byrd in "bedfellows" was not entirely carnal, for he, like Beverley, believed that miscegenation was the best solution to white-Indian con-flict. He felt that from the beginning of such contact the Indians had distrusted the English because they would not "inter-marry with them." Thus, he wrote:

Besides, morals and all considered, I cannot think the Indians were much greater heathens than the first adventurers, who, had they been good Chris-tians, would have had the charity to take the only method of converting the natives to Christianity. For, after all that can be said, a sprightly lover is the most prevailing missionary that can be sent amongst these or any other infidels.[11]

The Englishman noted the division of labor among the In-dians and stated that women did all the "work" while men engaged "only in the gentlemanly diversions of hunting and fishing." He also reported that only boys were still using bows and arrows, the men having adopted firearms. He thought the practice was beneficial to the whites because Indians were dependent upon Europeans for their

[10] *Ibid.*, 82, 218.
[11] *Ibid.*, 160, 218–19. On Byrd's advocacy of intermarriage, see also *ibid.*, 221–22.

weapons and because in warfare the swift, silent arrow was often more effective than the firelock. He ended his account of the visit with praise for the attempts that had been made to educate and Christianize the Virginia Indians. But he realized that little permanent change had been made. Indeed, he reported that the only success of Mr. Charles Griffin's efforts among the Saponi Indians was "to make them something cleanlier than other Indians are."[12]

In his account of the later meeting with a party of Saponi Indians, Byrd returned to white efforts to help the red men. The Indians at Fort Christanna were actually remnants of the Saponi and Tutelo tribes which were relocated upon the urging of Governor Alexander Spotswood. In the 1740's these Indians moved north and became a part of the Cayuga Nation within the League of the Iroquois. He believed that the plan of Governor Spotswood to settle the natives at Fort Christanna and to provide Griffin as teacher and minister would have succeeded had not the Indians been "debauched" and "ruined" by the whites. Byrd especially condemned the furnishing of rum to the natives. He thought that the Indians had moved northward because of an incident involving rum. While drunk, an Indian murdered another and was later hanged. The Indians seemingly had a great dislike and fear of this form of execution and thereupon left Virginia.[13]

The writer's other remarks on the Saponi were brief. He sought to impress his readers with the Indians' honoring the Europeans by coming to meet them on horses rather than on foot. He explained that the Indians had ridden "but three miles and 'tis likely they had walked afoot twice as far to catch their horses." Along with "all the grandees of the Saponi nation," four young women, whom the writer considered cleaner and more beautiful than most "copper-colored beauties," came to see the commissioners. The women were

[12] *Ibid.*, 219–21.
[13] *Ibid.*, 244–46, 314–15; Douglas L. Rights, *American Indians in North Carolina*, 114–15; and Leonidas Dodson, *Alexander Spotswood, Governor of Colonial Virginia, 1710–1732*, 74–96.

prostitutes, and despite their "charms" the whites sent them away, although Byrd wrote that "a princess for a pair of red stockings can't, surely, be thought buying repentance much too dear." He also noted that the women rode astride their horses, and despite the purpose of their visit they "were so bashful about it [the method of riding] that there was no persuading them to mount till they were quite out of our sight."[14]

A few years later William Byrd II made another journey and from the experience produced another work which contained a few indications of the life of the native Americans. In 1733 Byrd and a party of ten other whites, three or four Negro servants, and three Indian guides made a trip westward to inspect a large tract of land that Byrd had purchased. The land, which was located at the junction of the Dan and Irvine rivers immediately south of Virginia in North Carolina, was called "Eden" by its owner, and his short description of the area and the party's travels was designed to encourage settlers and buyers. In the *Journey to the Land of Eden*, as the work was entitled, the few items regarding Indians dealt with aspects of native civilization that a curious European might find interesting. At one point in the journey the party came upon a "papa Tree," and Byrd wrote of the tree's value to the Indians. The wood was dried and used to produce fire. According to the author, two sticks of "papa Tree" wood were rubbed together, and within a few minutes fire was easily produced. He also used the occasion to observe that the red men never used an old fire in their sacrifices but always kindled a new one. Another day, an Indian demonstrated the native method of swimming. Byrd commented that the Indians "strike not out both hands together, but alternately one after the other, whereby they are able to swimm [*sic*] both farther and faster than we do." Elsewhere in the work, Byrd repeated his criticism of the native men for being lazy. He believed that the male's only occupation consisted of hunting, while the female was forced to "labor." Evidently the Englishman had inquired about the division of labor, for he reported that the Indians believed that it was

14 Byrd, *Prose Works*, 314, 317.

the "fault" of women that work had originally been given to mankind. In this case Byrd did not note the similarity between the Indians' belief and that of orthodox Christianity.[15]

From his comments it is apparent that William Byrd II was a sympathetic observer of the native Americans. Despite the disagreement of Robert Beverley II with the history of Virginia written by Oldmixon who received his information from Byrd, the brothers-in-law shared an admiration for the Indian and held a common belief in intermarriage as the best solution to end conflict between the two races.

At least one other Virginia contemporary of Beverley and Byrd also believed in the benefits of intermarriage between European and Indian. The Reverend Mr. Peter Fontaine, who was Byrd's parish minister and who acted as chaplain for the boundary commission, praised white and Indian miscegenation but condemned white-Negro mixing. The minister believed that any white-Indian alliances should be on a permanent basis, and he strongly criticized English traders who had children by "squaws alias whores" and then deserted the off-spring. Fontaine also offered a possible reason for the rarity of white-Indian marriages. He noted that the Council of Virginia suspected John Rolfe of treason in his marrying the Indian "princess" Pocahontas. The clergyman felt that the Council's disapproval probably prevented the growth of what he considered a worthy practice.[16]

The extent of contact that Fontaine had with Indians is unknown, although as a member of the boundary commission he would have had an opportunity to observe the Indian guides. But his older brother, John or Jacques Fontaine, left more complete accounts of two meetings with the Indians of Virginia.

In 1715 John Fontaine was sent to America by his family, which was interested in coming to the New World. He landed in Virginia and traveled widely in the colony seeking suitable land. In November, 1715, Fontaine spent several days at the home of Robert

[15] *Ibid.*, 28, 385, 388, 391, 397, 403, 413.
[16] Jacques Fontaine, *Memoirs of a Huguenot Family*, trans. and ed. Ann Maury, 349–50.

Beverley and attempted to purchase some of Beverley's land. Instead of selling the three thousand acres Fontaine desired, Beverley wanted to lease the land for 999 years, but the offer was refused. Fontaine later traveled to New York City and then returned to Virginia, where he was able to purchase a "plantation." The other members of the family soon joined him in Virginia.[17]

During his visit in Virginia, Fontaine had two opportunities to observe the natives. Soon after his arrival he passed "by the side of the road an Indian cabin." The Englishman stopped and inspected the rude dwelling and its inhabitants. He noted that the structure was about seven feet high with walls of upright logs and with a bark roof. The furnishings consisted of a sleeping mat of "bulrushes" and a single iron pot. The traveler made no remark regarding any Indian man, but the strange appearance of the women attracted his attention. In his journal he wrote that "the Indian women were all naked, [wearing?] only a girdle they had tied around the waist, and about a yard of blanketing put between their legs, and fastened one end under the fore-part of the girdle, and the other behind."[18]

In the spring of 1716 John Fontaine joined a party of Englishmen led by Governor Alexander Spotswood that was on its way west to gain firsthand knowledge of the possibility of expansion over the mountains.[19] On their journey the travelers stopped for a short time at Fort Christanna. Fontaine made lengthy comments on the brief visit but most of the remarks dealt with the easily observed aspects of the Indians' life. He stated that the red men numbered only about two hundred and were greatly dependent upon the English. They paid an annual tribute to the Virginia government for providing protection against hostile natives. The brevity of the native costume

[17] *Ibid.*, 238, 247, 265–70; and Wright, *First Gentlemen of Virginia*, 307.
[18] Fontaine, *Memoirs*, 264.
[19] Discussions of the trip and the members of the party, who have become known in history as the "Knights of the Golden Horseshoe," may be found in Dodson, *Alexander Spotswood*, 238–40, and Delma R. Carpenter, "The Route Followed by Governor Spotswood in 1716 Across the Blue Ridge Mountains," *Virginia Magazine of History and Biography*, Vol. LXXIII (Oct., 1965), 405–12.

caused comment on this occasion as it had earlier. The common dress of the Indians was a blanket tied about the waist, but Fontaine did note that some wore a deerskin "over the shoulders like a mantle." A coating of "bear oil" was worn on the body, and the faces of the warriors were painted a vivid red and blue. The writer praised the general appearance of the red men and believed that the erect posture resulted from the use of a cradle board. He did not describe the device but indicated that the native child was confined to it during the first two years of life.[20]

Unlike William Byrd II, who a few years later complained of the chastity of the Fort Christanna Indian women, Fontaine praised the women for being "very modest" and exceedingly faithful to their husbands. He reported that monogamy was the rule but that a man might marry a second wife if the first were to "grow so old that she cannot bear any more children." He also briefly mentioned other aspects of native culture. He implied that although the Indians had previously been ruled by a "king," they were governed by a council of twelve at the time of his visit. He noted that the family dwellings were often joined together to form a circle and that the houses contained few utensils except for wooden dishes. The Englishman observed sweat houses or "ovens" located between the village and a nearby stream, but he made no comment as to the use of the "ovens." The Indians entertained their guests with an archery contest and a "war dance" by the boys. Fontaine was not favorably impressed by the dance. After commenting that the rhythm was provided by striking a board with two sticks, he added that the participants sang or rather "shrieked hideously."[21]

Fontaine's impression of the Indians at Fort Christanna was one of disapproval. Except for the chastity and physical appearance of the native Americans, he found nothing to praise. He believed that the Indians lived "as lazily and miserably as any people in the

[20] Fontaine, *Memoirs*, 270–74, 276–78.
[21] *Ibid.*, 273–79.

world."[22] If Fontaine had any thoughts as to the reason for the sloth-fulness, he did not record it in his journal.

Four men left fairly long accounts of the Indians of early eighteenth-century Virginia. Robert Beverley II and Hugh Jones were the more systematic, but Beverley and William Byrd II wrote at more length. Beverley and Byrd had the greatest personal knowledge. Each of these men had contact with the natives on several occasions during his lifetime. John Fontaine's account was based on two rather brief encounters. Jones mentioned seeing only one group of Indians, those at Fort Christanna, and this sojourn was probably the man's only personal contact. Interestingly, each of these four men visited the pacified Indians at Fort Christanna. Some of their comments dealt with the same native society and culture during a relatively brief period of time.

The interest and the attitude of the travelers was not uniform. Beverley's account included numerous details of the ceremonial life of the red men. Byrd related several of the native myths. Fontaine and Jones were critical of the native Americans, and Jones's condemnations were extreme. Beverley and Byrd had an appreciation and sympathy for the Indians. They condemned the effect of the white and his culture on the native, and along with Peter Fontaine, they believed that much of the trouble between white colonists and Indians could have been prevented if Europeans had accepted intermarriage. John Lawson, a contemporary of these men, also advocated white-Indian marriages. From his extensive knowledge of the natives of the Carolinas, Lawson wrote a highly useful account of the Southern Indians.

[22] *Ibid.*, 277.

VI

John Lawson: Perceptive Traveler
Among the Carolina Indians

MONG the observers of the Southern Indians during the first half of the eighteenth century, few, if any, equalled John Lawson in the extent of interest and depth of perception of native civilization. Indeed, if all accounts of the Indians of the Carolina Piedmont except Lawson's were lost, those Indians and their culture would still be known with a high degree of accuracy. The value of the Englishman's observations is somewhat surprising, because he was seemingly without any experience among Indians when he began the journey upon which his work was based. According to Lawson, his knowledge of the Carolina natives was gained from an extensive trip which he made very soon after his arrival in the New World in 1700. It seems probable, however, that he supplemented his information during his work as a surveyor between 1701 and 1708, when he returned to England to secure publication of his writing.

Very little is known of Lawson's background, but apparently he came to the colonies as the result of a whimsical desire to travel. In 1700 he went to New York and after a short time traveled to Charles-Town, South Carolina. On December 28, 1700, he joined a party of six Europeans and four Indians, probably interested in the fur trade. He traveled by canoe to the mouth of the Santee River, near present-day Columbia. The companions then turned northward, following a well-established Indian trading path. Lawson crossed most of North Carolina, concluding the journey with only one Indian guide, because one of the Englishmen returned to Charles-Town and the others went directly to Virginia. Lawson left the trail and turned east near present Hillsboro to travel directly to the settlements in eastern North Carolina. In February, 1701, after having walked "a thousand miles," he arrived at the home of Richard Smith on the "Pampticough River." Lawson apparently became a deputy-surveyor in the colony and in 1705 was one of the incorporators of Bath. In 1708 he sailed to England, probably to supervise the publication of his account of the Carolinas. In 1709 *A New Voyage to Carolina* appeared in London, and before the author returned to America, he secured the position of surveyor-general of the northern colony of the Carolina Proprietors.[1]

A New Voyage to Carolina was divided into four sections, two of which, "A Journal of a Thousand Miles" and "An Account of the Indians of North-Carolina," contained long, vivid descriptions of the natives. Lawson's comments ranged over many aspects of Indian society and culture. He made observations not only about the appearance of the red men, his warfare, and his religion, which many colonial writers did, but also about his reaction to the cleanliness of Indian homes and the wildness of the native dogs.

Lawson and his fellow travelers were usually well received by the Carolina Indians, although the author did condemn the "Wateree Chickarees" for trying to steal their possessions. Hospitality was more often the case, and the "Congerees," the "Waxsaws," the Santees, and the "Kadapau" or Catawba were specifically mentioned as making the whites very welcome. The Santees welcomed the party "with fat barbacu'd Venison," and the "King" of the "Kadapau" offered com-

---

[1] John Lawson, *New Voyage to Carolina*, 24, 53. Hugh T. Lefler believes that Lawson may have been "urged, or even hired" to make the voyage to the New World by James Petiver, a London apothecary and botanical collector. He also indicates that Lawson may have been sent on his trip into the Carolina interior by the Proprietors, but he does not indicate his source of information. Lefler, ed., *New Voyage to Carolina*, xi, xli. James H. Rand has suggested that Lawson traveled to obtain "historical and descriptive sketches" of the Indians, but there is nothing in *New Voyages to Carolina* to indicate any reason for the long journey. *North Carolina Indians*, 26.

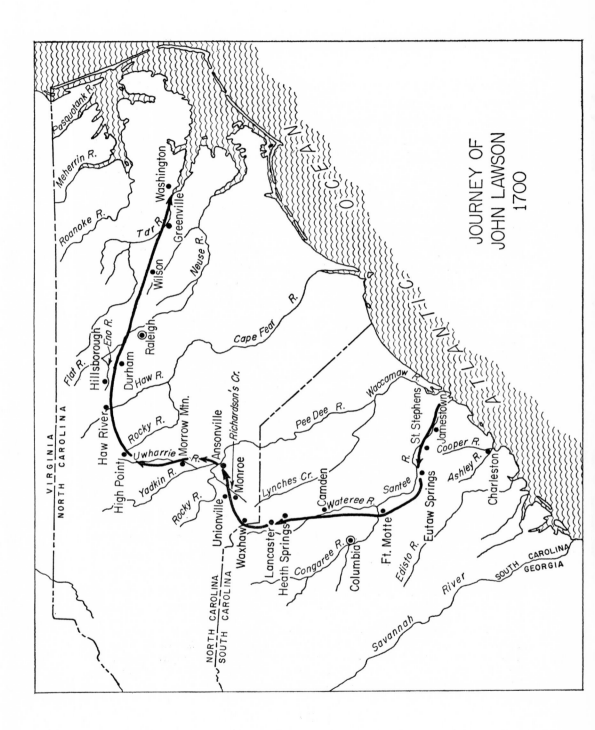

JOURNEY OF
JOHN LAWSON
1700

panions for the night. Despite the refusal of the English, the man and his wife were still gracious. Apparently the refusal came because the women were "Trading Girls" or prostitutes, for some of Lawson's associates had no aversion to Indian women. Before the incident, Lawson mentioned an Englishman being refused a companion for the night; but later, in another village, the same man had obtained "a pretty young Girl." Lawson, who refused similar offers throughout the trip, or at least made no mention of an acceptance, seemed pleased to report that the "pretty young Girl" left the man during the night, taking all his possessions, even his shoes. The writer's distaste for such arrangements seems to have been based on their promiscuous nature. Elsewhere in his account he proposed that "Ordinary People, and those of a lower Rank" be encouraged to marry native women as a means of improving white-Indian relations and hastening the conversion of the heathens to Christianity. Because Lawson and Robert Beverley II were among the very few authors to promote intermarriage between whites and Indians publicly and because Beverley's *History and Present State of Virginia* had been published in London only three years before Lawson's work, Lawson might have taken his idea from Beverley or been encouraged in his belief by the Virginian's statements. Nowhere, however, does Lawson indicate any familiarity with Beverley's writings, and the material relating to Indians is quite dissimilar.[2]

John Lawson made many comments about Indian dwellings and the Indians' subsistence activities. He described the homes as being made of bark and round like an "oven" with a fire hole in the top. The cabins must have been quite large, for several families lived in the same house. He did not find the cabins very comfortable. They were excessively warm, overrun with vermin, and some, like the houses of the thievish "Wataree Chickaree," were dark and smoky. He did

[2] Lawson, *New Voyage to Carolina*, 29–48, 237. A. L. Diket ignores Robert Beverley's published advocacy of intermarriage and concludes that Lawson's plea for "amalgamation" of the races was one of the few original thoughts in *New Voyage to Carolina*. "The Noble Savage Convention as Epitomized in John Lawson's 'A New Voyage to Carolina' " *North Carolina Historical Review*, Vol. XLIII (Oct., 1966), 429.

remark on the absence of a stench in the houses but could not explain the fact. He also noted that some of the villages were enclosed with palisades.

Lawson listed a wide variety of Indian foods. Besides venison, fish, bear, beaver, several fruits, and vegetables, some of the natives ate snakes, young wasps, turtles, and "Terebins." The native Americans had also begun to raise cattle and swine since the arrival of Europeans. To kill the larger wildlife, Lawson believed that Indians favored the use of fire. At one point in his journey he came upon some Sewee Indians burning a canebrake to drive out the deer therein. He also mentioned the use of disguises in hunting, a common practice among the Southern Indians. A hunter would attire himself in the head of a deer and stalk his prey. Lawson reported that there was minor danger in this practice, for occasionally the hunter would be killed by another Indian who believed the man to be a real deer. The English author made few observations on the preparation of food, but he did note that the Indians seldom removed the entrails of an animal before cooking. Once, the party was offered the meat of an unborn fawn, which had been cooked in its mother's "belly."[3]

Lawson believed that unlike the Iroquois whose women planted and cared for the corn, the Carolina Indian men had the responsibility for growing the crop. The Englishman also learned a little about the inter-tribal commerce in the area. On his way eastward to the North Carolina colony, he was accompanied by three "Enoe" Indians, and the party encountered a group of Tuscaroras. The Tuscaroras tried to prevent the Enos of the Catawba tribe from continuing, and Lawson believed that the reason for the Tuscaroran action was economic. According to him, they wanted to act as middlemen and sought to prevent English trade with interior tribes such as the Eno. Although Lawson did not indicate the use of "peak" or wampum, he did realize its importance among the Indians and devoted two pages to its description and the means of its manufacture.[4]

---

[3] *Ibid.*, 10, 22–23, 32, 49–53, 176–78, 206–207.
[4] *Ibid.*, 58, 188, 193–94.

A New Voyage to Carolina contained many references to the appearance of the Indians, especially of the women. Lawson noted physical differences even among closely situated tribes, but in general he described the natives as well-made, tall, and of a tawny color, which was increased by the application of bear's oil and a "darkening" material. The oil and the juice of "a scarlet root" were also rubbed on the hair. The Englishman noted that the red men usually removed their facial and body hair and that the "Keyauwee" were unusual in wearing whiskers. The "Waxsaw" custom of flattening the heads of male infants was also uncommon. This practice moved the eyes further apart than normal, Lawson said, and he indicated that the "Waxsaw" believed they were better hunters because the eye separation improved their vision. Despite his contention that the Indian was not really "robust," Lawson noted the absence of dwarfs and saw only one humpbacked person during his travels. The erect posture of the natives was attributed to the use of the cradle board. He praised the beauty of the Indian maidens, especially the appearance of the Congaree women, whom he stated smoked a great deal of tobacco. The women dressed their hair "like a Horse's Tail," and both sexes wore ear ornaments. The teeth of both men and women were yellowed by the habitual use of tobacco. Lawson noted that he never saw an Indian woman with "very large Breasts" and that they removed their pubic hair while men did not.[5]

Indian marriage and sexual customs seemed to intrigue Lawson. He stated that most girls married in their early teens, although among some of the tribes such as the "Waxsaw" the girls merely began to take lovers at that age. Marriage consisted mainly of the man's paying for the woman, but the union had to be approved by the girl's parents and by the village leader. Marriage between cousins was forbidden, but a man could marry two sisters or his brother's widow. Furthermore, Lawson thought that the natives sought to marry within their own tribe. Polygamy was approved, but in practice only a few of the better hunters and warriors had more than two wives. Divorce was

[5] *Ibid.*, 29–34, 53, 171–74, 190–92.

a simple arrangement, and a man could sell his wife and sometimes would oblige a friend "by letting her [the man's wife] out for a Night or two." In cases of adultery the man was punished by paying the offended husband, but the woman, who was considered "weak," escaped retribution. The author noted that English traders usually took Indian wives to care for them and assist them in learning the Indian language. The only criticism offered of such an arrangement was that the children belonged to the wife according to native custom and would be brought up as Indians. Although Lawson believed that native wives never scolded their husbands, he did castigate them as "mercenary" and upon occasion willing to sell their favors in the absence of their husbands. Prostitution was normally limited to a separate class of women, the "Trading Girls," who wore a distinctive hair style. These women were selected for their youth and beauty by the "King," who received most of their earnings. Later, "Trading Girls" could marry without dishonor unless they had a child, a misfortune that was condemned. Finally, a belief in European superiority was revealed in Lawson's opinion of the virility of the Indian. He thought that the native male was a "weak" lover and that the women preferred European men.[6]

Lawson was not as interested in other Indian social mores. He noted that a woman went into isolation for forty days following the birth of a child and that children were nursed until "they are well grown." He casually mentioned the absence of parental discipline and recommended that Indian children be given a European education, cautioning against the use of corporal punishment, which was against native custom. Lawson believed that the red man never stole from his people, although he did from the white man. Death was the usual punishment for murder, but sometimes the grieving relatives could be satisfied by a money payment.[7]

Considering the length of his discussion of Indian civilization, Lawson was not overly concerned with the political system or warfare

[6] *Ibid.*, 29–37, 183–88.
[7] *Ibid.*, 19–20, 189, 237–38.

of the Indians. He mentioned the presence of "kings" among all of the Indians that he visited in the Carolina Piedmont. He recognized that the monarchs' powers were usually limited: all warriors could freely express their opinion, and a majority made the final decision. Lawson noted that the "absolute" power of the Santee "king" was not common. Instead of actually ruling, the village leader acted as the group's spokesman and official host for visiting strangers. Succession to the "kingship" went to the son of the late "king's" sister, but the Englishman noted that the new leader needed village approval or he might be poisoned. The "Keyauwee" Indians explained the preference for matrilineal descent by saying that the mother never really knew who the child's father was! Lawson made very few comments regarding warfare, but he did describe the fate of prisoners. Enemies who had been captured were usually slowly killed by means of small slivers of wood which were inserted into the skin and then burned. Prisoners were sometimes spared to become slaves. To prevent escape, a slave's feet were crippled.[8]

The medical practice and religion of the Indians drew numerous comments from Lawson. Besides making scattered references to medicine in his "Journey," he devoted fourteen pages to the subject in his "Account" of the Indians. The red men that Lawson saw used a variety of curatives. Concoctions of plants and roots were administered to cause vomiting or to cure wounds and stomach-aches. When one of the Englishmen became crippled, he was cured by an Indian who scratched the swelling with snake teeth and applied a "sassafras" poultice. Later, Lawson saw the Tuscaroras use a similar treatment. In his opinion, the use of sweat houses was perhaps the most common Indian method of treating illness. Frequently, after the steam had thoroughly warmed him, the patient ran to a nearby stream and plunged into it. Much of the medical practice was handled by "Conjurers," and many of these men were believed to have supernatural power. The "King" of the "Saponas" [Saponi] was also a "Conjurer,"

[8] *Ibid.*, 18, 20, 44, 47, 51, 195–98, 225.

and he was said to have gone into a violent storm and calmed the winds in a very short time.[9]

Like the Reverend Mr. Francis Le Jau, Lawson noted a few Indian practices similar to Old Testament customs, but the observation of an offering of the first fruits and the practice of circumcision among one tribe did not lead Lawson to connect the red men and the Jewish people. He made no guess as to the origin of the Indians, but he did not believe the ones he visited were the oldest inhabitants of the New World. This conclusion was based on his finding pot shards unlike the pottery of the living Indians. Lawson found the Indians reluctant to discuss their religion, but he did learn that they had a concept of "good Spirits" and of "bad Spirits." He mentioned that they kept roosters for sacrificial purposes and set up idols in corn fields. His most vivid description of native religious life concerned the "Husquenawing," a puberty rite for both sexes, but particularly for boys. The ceremony was held at "Christmas" in a large, darkened cabin. The youths were made to fast and were given "intoxicating Plants." Afterwards, the young people could not or would not speak for some time. Lawson believed that the purpose of the ceremony was to teach obedience and to "harden" the participants. He also mentioned ceremonies in the spring and at harvest time. These rituals, along with celebrations of war and peace, consisted primarily of dancing. Accompaniment was provided with drums and gourd rattles. Lawson also noted the disappearance of sexual restraint following the harvest dance.[10]

Lawson described burial customs of the Carolina Indians. The European seemed surprised that an "Indian Funeral Sermon" was given before burial and that a wife did not mourn the loss of her husband, even though the man's blood relatives grieved and sometimes hired professional mourners. Lawson may have witnessed a Santee burial, of which he left a good account. The corpse was first treated with a mixture of herbs and bear oil and then placed in a "Tomb" with gifts and possessions. Later, the flesh was removed and

9 *Ibid.*, 10, 19–21, 42–43, 49, 60, 212–15.
10 *Ibid.*, 36–40, 56, 169–76, 210, 233–34.

the bones preserved for many years. A "Quiogozan," or idol, was placed in the tombs of some of the tribes' royalty. If a warrior was slain away from home, the body was covered with stones and each future passer-by added another stone. Lawson and his party found several of these mounds during the course of their travels.[11]

Throughout his book, John Lawson made comments that revealed the Indians' adoption of items and practices of European origin. At one point in his travels the Englishman questioned some unidentified Indians about their religious ideas. He was told of a belief in a soul and reward and punishment after death and a story of "a great Deluge." If the author recognized the possibility that revelations were at least partly due to European contact, he gave no indication in his writing. He praised the skill of his guide, "Santee Jack," in the use of a European weapon, but generally he felt that the Indians had suffered in their contact with white culture. The Indians had become overly fond of rum and sometimes became so intoxicated that one of them would fall into a fire. Lawson also commented that some of the Indians had learned to make English "White-Bread" and were using pieces of glass from bottles as arrow points.[12]

John Lawson was a sympathetic observer of the American Indian. He praised the patience, courtesy, and charity of the natives, believing that Europeans received much better treatment from the Indians than they gave in return. He did comment that Indians kicked and did not properly feed their dogs, which were so wild that Lawson incorrectly asserted that they were tamed wolves rather than canines proper.[13] It does seem that Lawson had at least some racial prejudice. His belief that Indian women preferred European men to Indian men and his mentioning only "Ordinary People and those of a lower Rank" in regard to marriage with Indians perhaps best indicate this conclusion.

While in London in 1708–1709 Lawson became acquainted with Christopher, Baron de Graffenried, a Swiss colonizer, and soon

[11] *Ibid.*, 21–22, 44, 46, 179–83.
[12] *Ibid.*, 11, 36, 39, 57–58, 202–203. [13] *Ibid.*, 37–38, 119, 178–79, 235.

aided the promoter in settling some six hundred Palatines at New Bern, North Carolina. This settlement, and other indications of English expansion into the West, aroused the hatred of the Tuscarora Indians. In 1711 Lawson and the baron were seized by Tuscaroras while on a surveying trip in the wilderness. The Swiss was able to secure his freedom, but Lawson was killed by the Indians, who seemingly held the surveyor especially responsible for the westward movement of the whites.

The writing of John Lawson ranks exceptionally high among colonial accounts of the Indians. In *New Voyage to Carolina*, notice was taken of the nearly standardized items such as the Indians' appearance, religion, dwellings, and subsistence activities, and the author's comments on medicine, marriage, and sexual customs were especially profound. For example, Lawson was one of the very few writers who mentioned the custom of isolating women following childbirth and of puberty rites among the Indians. Few colonial travelers among the Southern Indians between 1660 and 1763 equalled John Lawson in the value and usefulness of their observations. He had a sympathetic understanding of the red men and recorded unusual facets of native culture. Two other eighteenth-century travelers in the New World used Lawson's discussion of the Indians. John Brickell plagiarized Lawson, often verbatim.[14] Mark Catesby indicated that he took his material from Lawson, but he greatly condensed the surveyor's remarks.[15]

After the defeat of the Tuscaroras in 1713 and of the Yamassees a few years later, the British devoted their major efforts to the interior tribes, especially the Cherokees and the Creeks of the Piedmont and trans-Appalachian Southeast. British contact with these important tribes continued throughout the colonial period. But before a study can be made of the interior travelers, attention must be given to a final group of colonials who encountered a small band of coastal Indians.

[14] Percy G. Adams, *Travelers and Travel Liars, 1660–1800*, 149–57.
[15] *Natural History of Carolina, Florida, and the Bahama Islands*, II, VII–XVI.

VII

Early Georgia Colonists and the Indians

WITH the founding of Georgia came extended and prolonged contact between Englishmen and the Indians along the south Atlantic coast. The Georgia settlers were not the first whites to encounter these Indians. In the sixteenth century, Spaniards explored the area and maintained their contacts with the natives, especially after the founding of St. Augustine in 1565. The French also explored and made an unsuccessful attempt to settle on the St. Johns River. In the seventeenth century the red men more frequently encountered Europeans; there were not only the Spaniards but also English explorers and settlers of the Carolinas. The Virginia and Carolina fur and deerskin traders also sought the bounties of the Southern forests. With the arrival of the settlers, however, the nature of English-Indian contact in Georgia changed. No longer were the English visitors few in number and interested almost entirely in commerce with the red men; the new group sought permanent homes and permanent occupation of land claimed by the Indians.

Because of the danger posed by the Spanish and French to the new colony and because of the small number of settlers in the early years of settlement, the attitude of the Indians toward the Englishmen was exceedingly important. Fortunately, the native Americans proved to be friendly and helpful. From the beginning the Georgia Trustees demanded fair treatment of the red men, and relations with the Indians during the colonial period were unusually amicable. In less than four months after the initial settlement at Yamacraw Bluff on the Savannah River, a treaty was negotiated granting the English the right to occupy the Tidewater area and trade among the Indians. The Creeks, who exercised at least nominal sovereignty over the area, were pleased with the fairness of the Georgia government. Perhaps they were anxious to have competition offered the Carolinians, who until this time had a near monopoly on the English trade with the Indian confederation.[1]

The individual who implemented and enforced the colony's Indian policies was the dominant figure in early Georgia history, James Edward Oglethorpe. After playing an important role in securing the Trustees' charter, which designated him as one of the Trustees, the former general and member of Parliament led the first group of Georgia colonists to the New World. After a short stay at Charles-Town, where the Carolina officials and citizenry proved most co-operative, Oglethorpe and the settlers arrived at Yamacraw Bluff on February 12, 1733. They were greeted by two Indians who proved very helpful in the founding of the province. They were Tomochichi, mico or chief of the Yamacraws, and Mary Musgrove.

Tomochichi, the son of a Yamassee man and a Creek woman, apparently had been banished from his home among the Lower Creeks and with a few followers had settled at Yamacraw Bluff only a few years prior to the arrival of the English colonists.[2] The friendship of the Indian leader was valuable, because he acted as an intermediary

[1] The importance of Indian affairs in the minds of the Trustees may be seen in John Percival, Earl of Egmont, *Journal of the Earl of Egmont: Abstract of the Trustees' Proceedings for Establishing the Colony of Georgia, 1732–1738*, ed. Robert G. McPherson.

[2] The ancestry of Tomochichi (Tomachichi, Tomo-Chi-Chi, Toma Chi Chi) has not been firmly determined, nor has the reason for his banishment. David H. Corkran believes his father was Yamassee and his mother Creek and that he was expelled because of the general Creek-Yamassee break in 1728. *Creek Frontier, 1540–1783*, 82–83. Frederick W. Hodge, ed., *Handbook of American Indians, North of Mexico* (2 vols.; BAE *Bulletin 30*), II, 776, 986, and Swanton, *Early History of the Creek Indians*, 108–109, believe that he was Creek, but Swanton stated that he might have been Yamassee. For an older study of him, see Charles C. Jones, Jr., *Historical Sketch of Tomo-Chi-Chi, Mico of the Yamacraws*.

between Oglethorpe and the Lower Creeks. Indeed, the promptness with which the general was able to meet with the Creek leaders and their willingness to grant the Tidewater region to the English was due to a considerable degree to Tomochichi. Mary Musgrove was a half-Creek, half-white woman who had married a "renegade" Carolina trader, John Musgrove. Her knowledge of Muskogean—the language of the Creeks—and of English and the fact that her mother's family was influential among the Lower Creeks proved most helpful to the white settlers.[3]

From his contacts with Tomochichi and the Yamacraws and his conferences with other Indians, Oglethorpe must have acquired an adequate if perhaps superficial knowledge of this information. There were probably two reasons for the scarcity of Indian data in his works and letters. First, his public responsibilities demanded much of his time and effort, and his writings concerning Georgia reflected a definite purpose rather than providing leisurely commentaries upon the colony and its European and native inhabitants. Second, Oglethorpe was aware of the keen interest in England in the colony and therefore stressed the friendliness of the Indians, their desire for Christianity, and their morality and virtue.

Oglethorpe's attitude toward Indians, formed before any actual contact with them, was expressed in *A New and Accurate Account of the Province of Georgia*, published in London in 1732. In the work, Oglethorpe, who may have had one or more collaborators, used Spanish and French writings but depended primarily upon John Archdale.[4] The promoter seemingly was concerned with lessening fears of prospective settlers by noting that Georgia contained few Indians and that smallpox and drunkenness were killing many of them. He hastened to add, however, that only the "vulgar" believed that most Indians were drunkards. For his description of the appearance of the

[3] For Mary Musgrove, see E. Merton Coulter, "Mary Musgrove, 'Queen of the Creeks': A Chapter of Early Georgia Troubles," *Georgia Historical Quarterly*, Vol. XI (Mar., 1927), 1–30, and Corkran, *Creek Frontier*, 82–84 *et passim*.

[4] Found in *Collections* of the Georgia Historical Society, I, 42–78, the source used in this study. See also Verner W. Crane, *Promotion Literature of Georgia*, 7–8.

red men, which attracted the attention of most Englishmen, he quoted a paragraph from Archdale and indicated that he agreed with the Carolina writer that the "tawny" color of the natives resulted from their use of oils and from the sunlight.[5]

Upon his arrival in America, Oglethorpe began a lengthy correspondence with many persons in Great Britain, especially with his fellow Trustees of the colony. Many of the letters mention Indians, but almost none of them give any indication of Oglethorpe's reactions to the natives or their culture and society.[6] In one of his early letters, the general mentioned the friendliness of the natives and their desire to become British subjects and learn of Christianity.[7] In "A Curious Account of the Indians by an Honorable Person," published in *A New Voyage to Georgia* by a "Young Gentleman," Oglethorpe reiterated his belief that the Indians truly desired to become Christians.[8]

In "A Curious Account" Oglethorpe also revealed other sentiments regarding the Indians. He felt that the major difficulty in converting them was one of communication and that once missionaries had mastered the natives' language, there would be little difficulty in teaching and saving them. He did, however, indicate that the Indians' love of rum and "the passion of revenge, which they call honor" were major obstacles "to their being truly Christians." But on other criteria he praised their morality: they hated adultery and disliked polygamy. He cited as evidence the fact that the punishment for adultery was for the offended husband to cut off the ears of the other man or kill him. Oglethorpe was correct in stating that adultery was condemned, but he was ignorant of or paid no attention to the considerable amount of polygamy that was found among the Creeks and other Southeastern Indians. He seems also to have erred in stating that in cases of adultery, only the man was punished. Unlike many other commentators,

[5] *New and Accurate Account*, I, 53–55.
[6] Most of the letters are printed in Ga. Hist. Soc. *Collections*, III.
[7] *Ibid.*, II, 380–81. Originally printed in Benjamin Martyn, *Account Shewing the Progress of the Colony of Georgia in America from its First Establishment.*
[8] London, 1735. In this study use has been made of the reprint of the work found in Ga. Hist. Soc. *Collections*, II, 37–66.

the general recognized cultural differences among Indians: Creeks were not thieves, whereas stealing was considered honorable among Uchees. Indians also condemned murder, but the term did not include killing an enemy or anyone who had "injured" them. "A Curious Account" concluded with a brief but accurate statement about native political organization. Oglethorpe realized that the "kings" of the Indians had no power to compel obedience but depended upon persuasion to gain support and compliance with their wishes. He also noted that in council meeting the opinions of the older men were most valued, although each warrior could express his view, and that decisions had to be unanimous before action could be taken.[9]

James Oglethorpe continued to have contact with the Southeastern Indians during his years in Georgia, but his later correspondence contained almost no descriptive material about them.

Among the original group of Georgia settlers was another individual who had at least a mild interest in the native people. Peter Gordon went to the colony as a minor official, remained a very short time, and returned to England. He paid another four-month visit to the colony in December, 1734, but in March, 1735, he returned to his homeland permanently. After he left America in 1735 he wrote a memoir of his two sojourns in the New World which was probably based on a diary or journal that he kept during those months.[10]

Gordon made a few brief references to the Indians. Upon the arrival of the settlers, he noted, the Yamacraws welcomed the whites with a salute of gunfire and a short dance. Gordon and a few other colonists spent the first night in Georgia at the Musgroves' trading post and were entertained with another dance. One of the Englishmen became inebriated and tried to join the Indians as they danced around a fire. Gordon, thinking that it would be better if the Indians did not see such "jollies and indiscretions," had the man physically removed from the celebration.[11]

[9] *Ibid.*, 61–62.
[10] *Journal of Peter Gordon, 1732–1735*, ed. E. Merton Coulter, 1–20.
[11] *Ibid.*, 35–36.

Later, Gordon attended a conference between Tomochichi and some of the Yamacraws and a group of Englishmen led by Oglethorpe. He commented that the Indians wore headdresses adorned with white feathers as an indication of their peaceful intentions. They smoked tobacco and blew the smoke to the left, right, up, and down. Gordon also observed the conference between Oglethorpe and the Creeks which formally granted the whites permission to settle along the coast, but his comments included no remarks on the native culture or his reaction to this important concession by the Indians.[12]

In 1734 Oglethorpe conducted to London a small party of Indians led by Tomochichi. The red men were objects of great curiosity in the British capital and no doubt whetted the interest of Englishmen in their newest possession, which needed financial support and able-bodied settlers.[13] Tomochichi and his party sailed home in October, 1734, but the colony's leader remained in England until late in 1735. Included in the party which sailed with Oglethorpe were Francis Moore, who recorded some impressions of the Indians, and a small group of Anglicans, who left their homeland for the avowed purpose of working for the salvation of the Georgia natives and the spiritual betterment of the white colonists.

Francis Moore became "keeper of the stores" at Frederica, a new southern settlement in Georgia, and in 1744 published his account of the early years of the colony's history. In the work, he exhibited some interest in the Indians, but his comments were primarily concerned with the importance of the natives to the English. Part of his record was based on hearsay. For example, Moore noted the importance of Tomochichi in aiding the first colonists to arrive in Georgia. He also related the almost continuous efforts of Oglethorpe to restrain England's Indian allies from attacking Spanish settlements in Florida. Francis Moore did observe a native dance and was impressed

---

[12] *Ibid.*, 43, 48–49.

[13] For an account of the Tomochichi party in England, see Egmont, *Journal*, 57–68, and Trevor R. Reese, "A Red Indian Visit to Eighteenth-Century England," *History Today*, Vol. IV (May, 1954), 334–37.

by the noise produced by the four drummers and the singing and shouting. He also noted the nearly naked, painted bodies of the dancers; however, Moore was even less interested in recording the red men's culture than were James Oglethorpe and Peter Gordon.[14]

In February, 1736, three particularly devout Anglicans arrived at Savannah. They were John and Charles Wesley and Benjamin Ingham. The men were united by more than personal friendship and the desire to aid the religious development of the new colony. They had attended Oxford University, and in 1732 Ingham had joined the small group of students and tutors organized by the Wesley brothers for methodical study and religious devotions. The group became known as the "Holy Club" or "Methodists." Each of the young men sincerely desired to labor among the Georgia Indians or the English settlers, but each also believed that the experience would further his own spiritual life and knowledge. A final common element among them was that none remained very long in the colony and none was satisfied by the results of his efforts.

The Reverend Mr. Charles Wesley remained in Georgia the shortest time—only six months. Unlike his brother John and Benjamin Ingham, Charles Wesley never expressed a desire to become a missionary to the native Americans. He went to Georgia as the Secretary of Indian Affairs and had the responsibility of issuing licenses to Indian traders.[15] Although he probably learned of native culture and society from the traders, he did not report any comments, nor did he record his own impressions of the Indians. He observed the red men more than once. He was present when Tomochichi and a few of his followers greeted the English upon their arrival in February, 1736, and shortly before he left Savannah he acted as recorder for a conference between Oglethorpe and some Creek leaders. He also may have seen some Indians while living at Frederica, but he made no men-

[14] *A Voyage to Georgia, Begun in the Year 1735* (London, 1744), reprinted in Ga. Hist. Soc. *Collections*, I, 79–152.

[15] Charles Wesley, *Journal of the Rev. Charles Wesley: The Early Journal, 1736–1739*, ed. John Telford, 59, 65–66.

tion of them in his journal.[16] In July, 1736, Charles Wesley left Georgia, and after a pleasant if unanticipated visit to Boston he returned to England in December, 1736. Although he later indicated a willingness to return to Georgia as a full-time minister rather than as a secretary, he soon became completely involved in his work in Great Britain and never returned to the New World.[17]

The Reverend Mr. Benjamin Ingham remained in America for more than a year and exhibited great determination to work among the Indians. Ingham's only known comments concerning his venture in Georgia were contained in a long letter written to his mother on May 1, 1736.[18] He spoke of his initial reluctance to leave home, his decision to go because of the persistence of John Wesley, and his desire to remove himself from the many "temptations" of England. He also described Tomochichi's friendly greeting of the party on its arrival. On another occasion, he met two native hunters and traded wine and biscuits for venison. He concluded his letter by expressing a desire to teach young Indians, especially the "young prince," Tonahowl, but he recognized some of the problems involved. Besides the "prince's" being "corrupted and addicted to drunkness," Ingham noted that the natives used no corporal punishment in their educational process and questioned his own ability to do likewise.[19]

Ingham attempted to remove one barrier to successful missionary work, that of communication. For several months he lived at the Musgrove trading post in order to learn the language of the Creeks; and he made progress in that endeavor, according to John Wesley. While learning the dialect, he also taught the native children in a school near the Yamacraw village. Tomochichi encouraged the

[16] *Ibid.*, 11, 65. Hugh T. Lefler errs in stating that Charles Wesley recorded his impressions of the Indians. *Travels in the Old South*, I, 136–37. The bibliography states that Charles went buffalo hunting with them, but Oglethorpe was the hunter.

[17] Charles Wesley, *Journal*, 66–96; and Egmont, *Journal*, 214.

[18] Luke Tyerman, *Oxford Methodists: Memoirs of the Rev. Messrs. Clayton, Ingham, Cambold, Hervey, and Broughton*, 63–80.

[19] *Ibid.*, 64–66, 75–80. Berkhofer notes the conflict that arose from the use of corporal punishment by whites and the Indians' dislike of such disciplinary means. *Salvation and the Savage*, 41–42.

missionary's efforts, but after he returned to England the school presumably disappeared.[20]

The last report of Ingham's activities in the colony was by John Wesley in February, 1737. In a letter to a college friend, he mentioned that Ingham was still living near the Yamacraw village a few miles outside Savannah, but he did not indicate the extent of his young colleague's activities nor the missionary's success. Soon afterwards, Benjamin Ingham returned to England for reasons which are not entirely apparent. Egmont reported that Ingham informed the Trustees that he returned "to take Priests orders," but Wesley stated that Ingham went home to seek recruits for the missionary efforts in the colony. Whatever the reason, Ingham did not return to America, despite his statement that he desired to do so. He soon broke with the Wesleys and associated himself with the Moravians. His departure ended the only real attempt by the English to work among the Georgia Indians during the 1730's.[21]

John Wesley began his work in Georgia with great confidence. In a letter written only a few days before his departure for America, Wesley was very enthusiastic about the opportunity to convert the heathens in the New World. In the same letter he also revealed the other major reason for his going to the colony; indeed, for him the primary reason was that of saving his "own soul." His missionary activity among the uncorrupted natives would, he hoped, permit him to "learn the purity of that faith which was once delivered to the saints."[22] Just as the early Christians labored among "heathens," Wesley wished to work among the heathen Indians. Yet, despite this strong desire, he was actually appointed and paid to minister to the colonists. Probably neither he nor the Trustees foresaw any great

[20] John Wesley, *Letters of the Rev. John Wesley, A.M.*, ed. John Telford, I, 211; and Egmont, *Journal*, 216.

[21] *Ibid.*, I, 277, 291; John Wesley, *Letters*, I, 228–29; John Wesley, *Journal of the Rev. John Wesley, A.M.*, ed. Nehemiah Curnock, I, 321; and John Percival, Earl of Egmont, *Diary of Viscount Percival, Afterwards First Earl of Egmont*, ed. Historical Manuscripts Commission, III, 80–81.

[22] John Wesley, *Letters*, I, 188; and Martin Schmidt, *Young Wesley: Missionary and Theologian of Missions*, trans. L. A. Fletcher, 21–22 *et passim*.

difficulty in his doing both. In reality, he was to enjoy no success among the Indians and made little effort to Christianize them.[23]

The small group of Indians who, led by Tomochichi, welcomed Oglethorpe upon his return were the first that Wesley saw. The minister noted that three of the red men, including the chief, wore European clothing, but despite his costume, Tomochichi had painted his face, wore beads in his hair, and had attached a "Scarlet feather" to one ear. The women of the party presented the whites with a jar of milk and another of honey. Wesley believed that the gifts were symbolic. If one would only treat the Indians as "children," they would be as sweet as "honey." Wesley was also encouraged by the words of Tomochichi. The old chief personally welcomed the clergyman for bringing "the great word" to his people but admitted that the Indians were somewhat confused about Christianity. The rivalry between Great Britain, Spain, and France confused them even more. Perplexed though he might be by the rivalry among the Christian colonizers, he shared the British antipathy toward the Spanish and their attempt to convert the natives. Wesley recorded the chief's sentiments in his journal. He wrote:

But we [the Indians] would not be made Christians after the Spaniards way to make Christians. We would be taught first, and then baptized. All this he [Tomochichi] Spoke with much earnestness, and much action both of his hands and head, and yet with the utmost gentleness both of Tone and manner.[24]

Wesley was heartened by Tomochichi's attitude. It does not

[23] Wesley's ministry in Georgia has been the subject of historical controversy. A recent article emphasizes the importance of the work on his later religious development. William B. Cannon, "John Wesley's Years in Georgia," *Methodist History*, Vol. I (July, 1963), 1–7. A most critical study is E. Merton Coulter, "When John Wesley Preached in Georgia," *Georgia Historical Quarterly*, Vol. IX (Dec., 1925), 317–51. No truly sound scholarly biography of Wesley has been written. The most thorough twentieth-century studies have been done by John S. Simon, but he deliberately ignores Wesley's contact with the Indians, and in his few comments, he reveals a total lack of sympathy with, or understanding of, the natives. *John Wesley and the Religious Societies*, 127–28.

[24] The meeting is described in John Wesley, *Journal*, I, 159, and in Egmont, *Journal*, 131–32. The quote is taken from the latter account, which is probably a transcription of a manuscript copy of Wesley's journal to which Egmont had access.

seem to have bothered him that the old chief had learned his prejudice against the Spanish and Catholics from the English.

The optimism of the young missionary soon changed to disillusionment and bitter animosity toward the Indians for several reasons. Wesley came to America to labor among the Indians, but he was unable or unwilling to undertake the task. From personal observation and from information furnished by men who had had long contact with the Southern natives, he found his belief in the simple, unsophisticated "heathen" to be naïve and incorrect. The entire Georgia ministry of John Wesley was one of controversy, strife, and disappointment.

In the summer of 1736, Wesley wanted to leave the English settlements on the coast and begin his work among the Indians, but Oglethorpe refused permission. The denial was made partly because of the fighting between the Chickasaws, whom Wesley then felt were the best prospects for missionary work, and the Choctaws and their French allies. But Oglethorpe's major consideration was the need for a minister in Savannah. In July, Oglethorpe wrote the Trustees requesting more ministers and indicating his fear of the settlers becoming "entirely destitute" should Wesley and Ingham both become active among the Indians. When Oglethorpe returned to England late in 1736, he again admonished Wesley not to leave the Georgia settlers.[25]

The personal contacts that Wesley had with the native Americans were with the Yamacraws and the groups of red men who visited Savannah. In June and July of 1736, parties of Chickasaws traveled to the new colony. Wesley had several conferences with them and was especially interested in their religious ideas. He learned that they believed in "4 Beloved things above, the Clouds, the Sun, the Clear Skie, and He that lives in the clear Skie, & Two with him, Three in all." The Indians also indicated that the "One" protected them from their enemies and that men had souls which existed after death. The majority of the Chickasaws evidently believed that the "Souls of Red

[25] *Ibid.*, 177; John Wesley, *Journal*, I, 238, 298; and John Wesley, *Letters*, I, 228–29.

Men . . . walk'd up and down after death near the place where their bodies lye, for they often heard cries and noises [near] the places where any prisoners had been burned," but one man "thought only the Souls of bad men walk'd, but that the good went up."[26] Wesley indicated no surprise at learning of the ill-defined Indian concept of a Trinity and a Heaven.

He wished to return with the Chickasaws to their home, but they refused him permission because they were at war and "had no time but to fight." When peace was established, he would be welcome and could learn much more from the "Old Men of his [the Indian speaker's] nation." Wesley also learned that the "beloved One" chose each of the "Old Men" as a child and taught him so that he had special knowledge. Despite the refusal, Wesley was impressed with the Chickasaws. In September, 1736, he wrote to John Vernon, one of the Trustees of the colony, and expressed his hope of learning the Chickasaw language. He praised these Indians as "humble and peaceful" and admired them because they had "so firm a reliance on Providence, so settled a habit of looking up to a Superior Being in all the occurrences of life."[27]

Wesley's comments about the Chickasaws were his last favorable remarks on the American Indians. By the time of his correspondence with Vernon, he had already been rebuffed in his attempt to convert the Yamacraws. On one occasion, when the minister pressed Tomochichi to become a Christian, the old chief heatedly replied, "Why these are Christians at Savannah! Those are Christians at Frederica! Christians drunk! Christians beat men! Christians tell lies! Me no Christian."[28] Further disillusionment came from persons who had intimate knowledge of the Southern Indians. In the summer of 1737 he talked with a Frenchman who had lived among the Choctaws. He recorded the Frenchman's belief that the gods of the red men were actually devils. After noting the man's account of native cruelty, the

[26] Egmont, *Journal*, 177–78.
[27] *Ibid.*, 178; and John Wesley, *Letters*, I, 228–29.
[28] Quoted in Jones, *Tomo-Chi-Chi*, 103.

minister added his own comment: "See *the religion* & *Nature truly delineated*!" Wesley had not always had such an adverse opinion of the Choctaws; in the previous year, he had stated that he believed that the Choctaws were "the least corrupted" of all Indians.[29]

By the time John Wesley changed his attitude toward the Choctaws, he had become one of the protagonists in a controversy that divided the small colony of Georgia. Wesley came to have tender affections for Sophia Hopkey, a young lady of eighteen to whom he taught French and whose religious devotion he sought to increase. Miss Hopkey indicated her desire for marriage. Oglethorpe and the girl's relatives in the colony urged the match, but after much soul-searching, Wesley hesitated, seemed to refuse, and began avoiding Sophia. He was advised against the marriage by his friends within the colony, and he still hoped to work among the Indians, which would have been impractical with a wife. Miss Hopkey hastily married one William Williamson at Purysbury, South Carolina. Wesley publicly noted that the marriage was questionable because proper bans had not been issued. He was privately hurt and confused. In August, five months after the marriage, Wesley refused Mrs. Williamson Holy Communion because in his opinion she was inattentive during church services, had refused to seek forgiveness for her sins, and had not given proper notice of her desire to partake of Communion.[30]

It was during the troubled summer of 1737 that evidence appeared of the change in Wesley's attitude toward the Indians. During this period his journal contained few references to them, but he had not forgotten the need for missionary activity. He had recently read David Humphreys' *Historical Account of the Incorporated Society for the Propagation of the Gospel in Foreign Parts* and believed that

[29] John Wesley, *Journal*, I, 238, 367–68.

[30] *Ibid.*, I, 355–95 *et passim*. The exact nature of Mrs. Williamson's offenses is not apparent. She had ceased to attend the study group organized by Wesley, and perhaps he still resented the omission of the bans prior to the marriage. All studies of Wesley's attraction to Miss Hopkey, his hesitation, and his disapproval of the marriage are essentially based on his journal. The letters he wrote while in Georgia and the Earl of Egmont's journal should also be consulted.

he had the solution to the problem of English missionary activity. In a July, 1737, letter to Humphreys, Wesley stated his belief that success among the natives would come only after "one or more" missionaries had been put to death for their faith. Such evidence of zeal would convince the stubborn Indians of the true belief of the English and also encourage other clergymen to continue the effort.[31]

John Wesley's final months in America were extremely contentious and disheartening. Immediately upon his denial of Communion to Mrs. Williamson, her husband brought charges of defamation against the minister. A grand jury indicted him on ten counts; one held that Wesley had pressed his attentions upon Mrs. Williamson, and the others were ecclesiastical in nature. Wesley was never brought to trial. Georgia officials said that business prevented the appearance of Williamson, a chief witness; but Wesley believed that his opponents were unwilling to face him in court. Despite a court order forbidding his departure, Wesley secretly left the colony on the evening of December 2, 1737. After going to Charles-Town, he sailed for home. In London the Georgia Trustees sought information regarding the controversy that had disrupted the young colony. Shortly after Wesley's return, the Trustees heard his testimony and found him innocent of the charges. Egmont believed that the minister had been "indiscreet" but thought that his adversaries were "much more to blame." But a few months later, after more details were known, the earl reported that the Trustees accepted Wesley's resignation "with great pleasure."[32]

Upon his departure from Georgia, Wesley made some general observations about the colony, and his conclusions regarding the American Indian were extremely bitter. He located and counted the number of fighting men for five tribes, but indicative of his disillusionment were his censorious characterizations of the natives. He began with general comments about their tendency to use stealth in warfare and their habit of scalping or removing the ears of victims. The only

[31] John Wesley, *Letters*, I, 225.
[32] Egmont, *Journal*, 107, 322–23, 331–33, 467, 481.

rule in Indian society was that each man sought "to do what he will, and what he can." They placed no real value on marriage, and the mother often killed the children if the father deserted the family. Indeed, according to Wesley, "whoredom they account no crime, and few instances appear of an Indian woman's refusing any one." He went on and on with his catalogue of their supposed vices. They were "gluttons, drunkards, thieves, dissemblers, liars" and "implacable, unmerciful, murderers of fathers, murderers of mothers, murderers of their own children; it being a common thing for a son to shoot his father, or mother, because they are old and past labor." Despite his earlier disapproval of them, Wesley stated that the Choctaws might possibly be an exception, but he did not elaborate on his reasons for excluding them from his general condemnation.[33]

Having made these remarks, the disappointed missionary proceeded to note some peculiar traits for most of the tribes mentioned. In addition to overindulging in food and drink, the Chickasaws were, said Wesley, lazy and excessively cruel to their captives. The Cherokees were as cruel as the Chickasaws and less courageous. They were also covetous. At times his invective surpassed his logic: while denouncing the Cherokees' intemperance, he said that they would not become inebriated unless the liquor were "on free cost." Uchees were deemed cowards, and Creeks did not know "what friendship or gratitude means." The Creeks were also highly opinionated and refused to learn new ideas, "least of all Christianity."[34] Wesley may have had the retort of Tomochichi in mind when he made the last comment.

The characteristics ascribed to the Southern Indians by John Wesley had little if any rational basis and contained little factual information but much malicious fancy. His personal observations were limited to the small group of Yamacraws near Savannah and the delegations of natives who visited the colony. Because of eager Europeans

---

[33] John Wesley, *Journal*, I, 407. It is perhaps needless to indicate that the Indians were guilty of few of the offenses attributed to them, but for a brief statement of the family life among these Indians, see Swanton, *Southeastern Indians*, II, 701–18.

[34] John Wesley, *Journal*, I, 408–409.

seeking to win and maintain the friendship of the Indians, some of the red men Wesley saw were perhaps lazy and corrupted, but the minister's emotional travail and his failure to engage in missionary activity among the Indians undoubtedly colored his impressions of the natives. Shortly after his return to England, he revealed the depth of his disappointment. In January 1738 he wrote:

It is now two years and almost four months since I left my native country in order to teach the Georgia Indians the nature of Christianity. But what have I learned myself in the meantime? Why, what I least of all suspected, that I, who went to America to convert others, was never myself converted to God.[35]

Within a few months Wesley was to undergo the famous experience that greatly altered his life and profoundly influenced the religious history of eighteenth-century England. Nevertheless, his observations about the native Americans were among the most unjust of any colonial traveler.

Philip Thickness, another traveler in early Georgia, had far different recollections of the Indians. In 1735 or 1736 Thickness, a lad of sixteen or seventeen, arrived in the new colony. He remained only a short time before returning to England. In London, he sought without success a post as ensign in a regiment Oglethorpe was raising for Georgia's defense. Thickness believed that his failure was due to Oglethorpe's displeasure. According to his account, he was examined by the Trustees about the state of the new province, and his "honest" answers displeased the colony's leader. He soon received a lieutenancy in a regiment stationed in Jamaica. Thickness later served in the Mediterranean and in 1753 became lieutenant-governor of Landguard Fort, Suffolk. Retiring in 1766, he spent the remainder of his life traveling, writing, and engaging in literary and legal disputes. In 1788 the first two volumes of his memoirs were printed in London.

The memoirs were an interesting mixture of anecdotes and reminiscences primarily designed to defend Thickness's conduct as a

---

[35] Quoted in *ibid.*, 176.

young officer in Jamaica. The reliability of the work concerning his visit to Georgia must be questioned for several reasons. The memoirs were written a half century after the trip, and the passage of time must have colored the memory of Georgia, which was excessively idyllic. Thickness related that he built a cabin in the forest and without care or difficulty supplied himself with all the necessities of life. There was no opposition to his isolated way of life, or in his words, "a true Robinson Crusoe line of life," and he nearly married a noble Indian maiden. But one day while "walking upon the margin of my creek, & playing upon the Flute," he had a vision of his mother. As he recalled "my Squa [*sic*];—my island;—my Robinson Crusoe plan, instantly lost all their claims," and he hastened home. Finally, it must be noted that the writer's understanding of natural history was none too good. He not only reported that a rattlesnake gained his first rattle only after living three years, but he also reported one snake that entered a hole tail first and said that rattlers could easily be killed with "the least stroke" on their heads.[36] Evidently Georgia rattlesnakes made a lasting impression on the Englishman, because he devoted more attention to them than to any other aspect of his residence in the New World.

Despite, or perhaps because of, the distortion of time and his romantic fancy, Philip Thickness made among the most interesting of any recorded comments about the Yamacraws. After relating his initial fright at the savage appearance of the natives, which he briefly noted as "their rude dress; painted faces, sliced ears; *nose bobs*! and tattooed skins," he found that he was entirely safe among Tomochichi's people. Indeed, he concluded that there was far more danger from the rattlesnakes than from the natives to one traveling in the forest. His favorable impression was probably furthered by his initial contact with the Yamacraws. He stated that on his first visit to the village, Tomochichi invited him to join in a feast of fresh oysters. Thickness also recorded an unusual native method of securing oysters. According to him, the Indians sometimes built fires over oyster beds at low tide and then enjoyed the roasted mollusks.[37]

[36] Philip Thickness, *Memoirs and Anecdotes of Philip Thickness*, I, 49–58, 64.
[37] *Ibid.*, I, 46–49.

Because the Englishman was fascinated by rattlesnakes, he mentioned two items in connection with them. He stated that the natives wore *"maugazeens"* of deerskin and covered their legs with leather for protection from snakebite. The "broad flaps" worn by the Indians were considered even more valuable by the author, because the snakes struck the "flaps" instead of the wearer. He also noted the Indian method of treating those unfortunate enough to be bitten. He wrote:

When the Indians are bitten, they tie a leather thong, tight above the wound, and their wives or children suck forth the poison, but not always with success, the limb swells immediately, & the patient dies in twenty-four hours, perhaps no remedy is of such good effect as olive oil, well & long fomented, with the patients own hands.[38]

Thickness had ambivalent feelings about his brief residence in Georgia. He had fond memories of his cabin and his visits with the Indians, but at one point in the narrative he characterized himself as "one of the foolish Georgia emigrants." Elsewhere, he was most critical of the effect of European civilization on the Indians. According to Thickness, the only contributions of the whites were *"diseases,* before unknown to them; [and] spirituous liquors, which render them frantic."[39] The young Philip Thickness found Georgia distasteful enough to leave after only a short visit, but as an old man he fondly remembered the gracious Yamacraws.

Several of the early Georgia colonists left brief accounts of their encounters with the Indians. Most of their observations dealt with the Yamacraws, a small portion of the Creek Confederation which settled near the Savannah River only a few years before the arrival of the Europeans. None of the writers had any real insight into the society and culture of the natives. Peter Gordon, Francis Moore, Charles Wesley, Benjamin Ingham, and Philip Thickness reported on the most superficial aspects of native life. The leader of the colony, General James Oglethorpe, revealed more of his attitude toward the

[38] *Ibid.*, I, 55–56.
[39] *Ibid.*, I, 23, 44.

Indians, but his brief comments were designed to secure support for the new venture.

The observations of John Wesley are especially interesting. Traveling to the New World for the purpose of converting the savages, the minister became bitter and frustrated. The Indians did not eagerly welcome his services as a missionary. This reluctance, his confused sentiments toward a young lady, and his disappointment following her marriage probably account for his harsh criticism of the Southern Indians. John Wesley was not the only colonial to experience failure in missionary activity among the Indians, but his condemnations were among the most unjust and unrealistic written by any British traveler.

During the period of Georgia's planning and settlement, several whites visited Indian tribes in the interior. Most of their contact was with the Cherokees and the Creeks, whose friendship was considered essential to the British colonies.

VIII

*Travelers Among the Southern
Indians, 1720–1739*

THE desire to improve relations
with the Southern Indians was frequently a reason for Englishmen to travel among them during the third and fourth decades of the
eighteenth century. These were important but troubled years in the
history of white-Indian relations in the Southern colonies. The long
period of relative peace which followed the Indian unrest during
Bacon's Rebellion had been broken by major uprisings of the Tuscaroras in 1711 and the Yamassees and their Creek allies in 1715. In the
1720's and 1730's neither the European settlers nor the natives were
certain about their relative positions. The imperialistic rivalry among
Great Britain, France, and Spain increased the uncertainty. The colonists and governments of each nation realized the importance of Indian allies and sought to continue old alliances and gain new ones.

The Southern Indians whose friendship the English most
eagerly sought were the Cherokees and the Creeks. The Tidewater
and Piedmont tribes between the Potomac and the Savannah rivers
had been depopulated by warfare, disease, and expulsion or corrupted
by European vices and pacified, and the English were free to turn
their attention westward.[1] The strengthening and maintenance of

---

[1] The disastrous effects of European culture on the natives were strongly denounced by F. Hall in 1731. Hall evidently had some personal contact with the Indians, but
he made few comments on the red men other than to condemn the effects of rum and un-

friendship were the major reasons for five men traveling in the Cherokee nation and the Creek confederation during the period. In 1725,
official positions held by George Chicken and Tobias Fitch required
them to visit these tribes. Two years later John Herbert wrote a brief
account of his travels among the Cherokees. In 1730 Sir Alexander
Cuming, one of the most interesting colonial travelers, made a hurried
trip through the Cherokee country, and in 1739 an anonymous writer
left his impression of the Creeks.

In 1725 George Chicken traveled west as Commissioner of
Indian Affairs for the colony of South Carolina. Before this trip
Chicken had other contacts with the Southern Indians. During the
Yamassee War, he had successfully led at least two small expeditions
of militia against the warring natives. Later, in the early 1720's, he
had served with John Herbert and William Bull as commissioners of
the Indian trade in the colony. Although the Commissioner was obli-
gated to make annual visits to the Indians, the reasons for the 1725
sojourn were more than routine. The French were becoming more
active among the Cherokees, traditionally allies of the English, and
the Cherokees and the Creeks, traditionally enemies, had been engaged in desultory warfare since the end of the Yamassee War. By the
mid-1720's the English were beginning to desire an end to war because of interruption of commerce. There was also fear that the two
nations might combine against the English, who had occasionally
excited one tribe against the other. Chicken sought to stifle Indian
sentiments for more trade with the French and a continuation of the
Creek war.[2]

scrupulous traders on the natives. *Importance of the British Plantations in America to this
Kingdom*, 57, 60–61, 85–87. On the decreasing numbers and importance of the Tidewater
and Piedmont Indians, see Nancy Oestreich Lurie, "Indian Cultural Adjustment to European Civilization," in James M. Smith, ed., *Seventeenth-Century America: Essays in
Colonial History*, 53, 55, and Douglas Summers Brown, *Catawba Indians: The People of
the River*, chaps. vi–vii *et passim*.

[2] The importance of the Cherokee trade with the English is indicated in Mary U.
Rothrock, "Carolina Traders among the Overhill Cherokee, 1690–1760," East Tenn.
Hist. Soc., *Publications*, Vol. I, (Jan., 1929), 3–18; W. Neil Franklin, "Virginia and the
Cherokee Indian Trade, 1673–1752," East Tenn. Hist. Soc., *Publications*, Vol. IV (Jan.,

On June 17, 1725, Commissioner Chicken left his home and traveled west on horseback. After passing through Fort Congaree, near present Columbia, South Carolina, he arrived at "Keewohee" or Keowee. There were at various times two or more Cherokee towns by that name. Chicken probably went to the one known as "Old Keowee," located near present Clemson, South Carolina. This was one of the principal towns of the Lower Cherokees. The Cherokees, who spoke dialects of the Iroquoian language, constituted the largest tribe in the Southeast. The nation was later commonly divided into three divisions: Lower, Middle and Overhills. Chicken and other colonists used the term "Upper Cherokees" to embrace both Middle and Overhill. The Lower Cherokees were located on the Keowee River and other upper tributaries of the Savannah River.

Upon Chicken's arrival, he was greeted by "King Crow" and other town leaders. After being led to the "most Publick Place in the Town," seated in a "Great Chair," and fanned with eagle feathers, he was formally welcomed by the Cherokees. After Chicken's reply, a salute was fired and he and the native leaders retired to a trader's house for the ceremonial smoking of tobacco. The commissioner was given similar welcomes at other towns during his travels.[3]

George Chicken's major concern was not the recording of the Cherokees' culture, and he spent much of his time seeking to increase the influence of pro-English leaders. The absence of a tradition of political coercion among the native Americans caused the Englishman considerable difficulty. King Crow of Keowee was an ally, but the commissioner realized that he could only persuade his people, not force them to act. At one point during his visit, Chicken complained about the slowness of efforts being made to fortify the town. The Cherokee leader plainly told him "that the people would work as they

1932), 3–21; and W. Stitt Robinson, Jr., "Virginia and the Cherokees: Indian Policy from Spotswood to Dinwiddie," in Darrett B. Rutman, ed., *Old Dominion: Essays for Thomas Perkins Abernethy*, 21–40.

    [3] "Colonel Chicken's Journal to the Cherokees, 1725," in Mereness, *Travels*, 97–98, 101–102, 110, 112; David H. Corkran, *Cherokee Frontier: Conflict and Survival, 1740–62*, 3; and Hodge, *Handbook of American Indians*, I, 674.

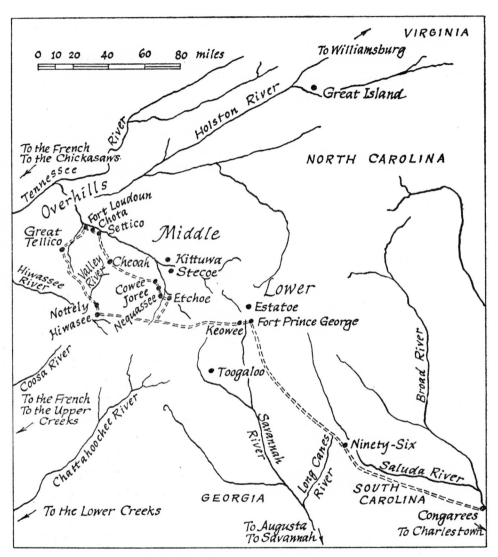

From The Cherokee Frontier, by David H. Corkran

The Cherokee Country, 1740–62

pleased and go to Warr when they pleased, notwithstanding his [King Crow's] saying all he could to them, and that they were not like White Men." On other occasions, the journalist complained of similar situations elsewhere in the nation, commenting that the Cherokee leaders were too much led by the people.[4]

Despite his preoccupation with official matters, the commissioner did make a few comments regarding the natives' way of life. He noted that "Great Terriquo," or Great Tellico, was unusual in having two "Town Houses," because it was settled by "people of Two towns." He added that because the town was greatly exposed to enemies, the people had "Enforted" and made "Muskett proof" the town houses and their own homes. Great Tellico, on the Tellico River in present-day Monroe County, Tennessee, was one of the westernmost Overhill Cherokee towns and therefore closer to the Chickasaws and Choctaws. The commissioner frequently noted the degree of protection offered by other villages.[5] Chicken also reported the "purifying" of a person returned from captivity. Such persons were detained for four days in the town house, and during the period men and women danced continuously. Chicken was not actually interested in the ceremony. He was making the point that some information received from a woman regarding the Creeks was probably accurate because she had been in the town house with a man returned from Creek captivity. A short time later, Chicken was at Keowee during the annual Green Corn Dance, but he made no observations on the ceremony.[6]

Chicken left Keowee on October 20, 1725, amid a salute of gunfire and arrived at his home in early November. During his nearly four months among the Cherokees he had made relatively few comments on the Indians other than those dealing with their attitude toward the English and England's policy in the area. Generally, he was impressed with the Cherokees and revealed no adverse judgments of any Southeastern Indians except the Chickasaws. He believed that

[4] Chicken, "Journal," 109, 111, 115–18, 126–31, 136, 153.

[5] *Ibid.*, 111–12, 149, 150.

[6] *Ibid.*, 121, 140.

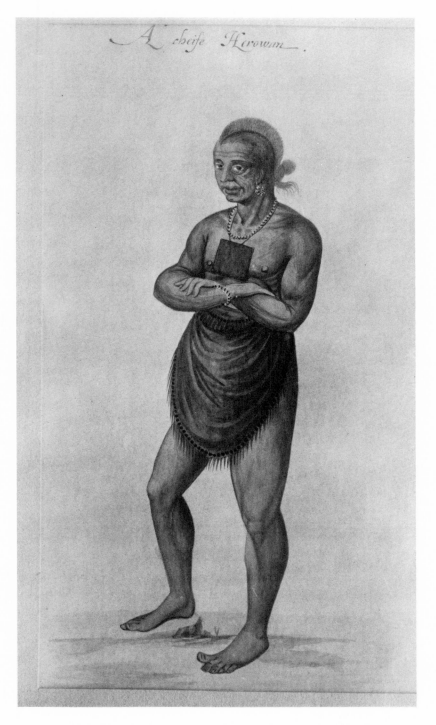

An Indian Elder or Chief. Watercolor by John White.
Courtesy of the Smithsonian Institution National Anthropological Archives, Bureau
of American Ethnology Collection

An Indian Woman and Child. Watercolor by John White.
Courtesy of the Smithsonian Institution National Anthropological Archives, Bureau of
American Ethnology Collection

Old Man in His Winter Garment.
Watercolor by John White.
Courtesy of the Smithsonian Institution National
Anthropological Archives, Bureau of American
Ethnology Collection

The Conjurer. Watercolor by John White. Encounters with Indian
shamans and conjurers were frequently related by the travelers.

The Manner of Their Fishing. Watercolor by John White.
Courtesy of the Smithsonian Institution National Anthropological Archives, Bureau of American Ethnology
Collection

Indians Dancing. Watercolor by John White.
Courtesy of the Smithsonian Institution National Anthropological Archives, Bureau of American Ethnology Collection

Within the illustration, the following handwritten labels appear:

The tipe...

Their grene corne

Corne newly sprong

Their sitting at meate

The place of solemne prayer

The house wherin the Tombe of their Herounds standeth

·SECOTON·

A Ceremony in their prayers wt strange iesturs and songs dansing abowt posts carued on the topps lyke mens faces.

Village of Secoton. Watercolor by John White. The houses are typical of the southeastern Algonquians.

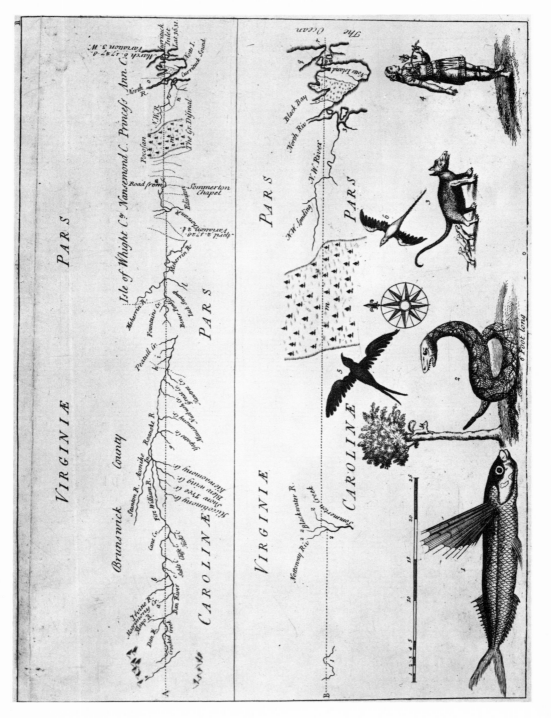

William Byrd II, *Virginia-Carolina Line*, ca. 1738.
Courtesy of the Curators of the Bodleian Library

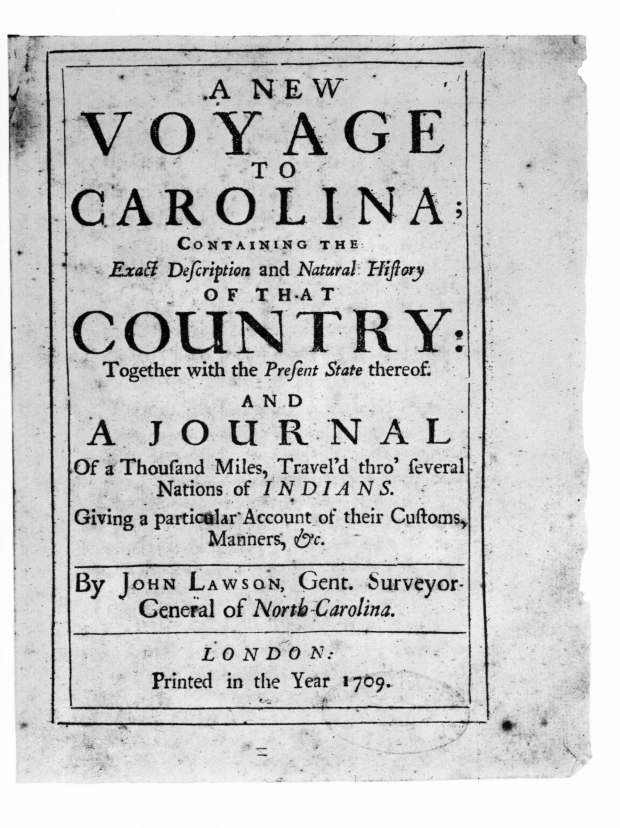

A NEW
VOYAGE
TO
CAROLINA;

CONTAINING THE

Exact Description and *Natural History*

OF THAT

COUNTRY:

Together with the *Present State* thereof.

AND

A JOURNAL

Of a Thousand Miles, Travel'd thro' several
Nations of *INDIANS*.

Giving a particular Account of their Customs,
Manners, &c.

By JOHN LAWSON, Gent. Surveyor-
General of *North-Carolina*.

LONDON:
Printed in the Year 1709.

Title Page of John Lawson, *A New Voyage to Carolina,* 1709.

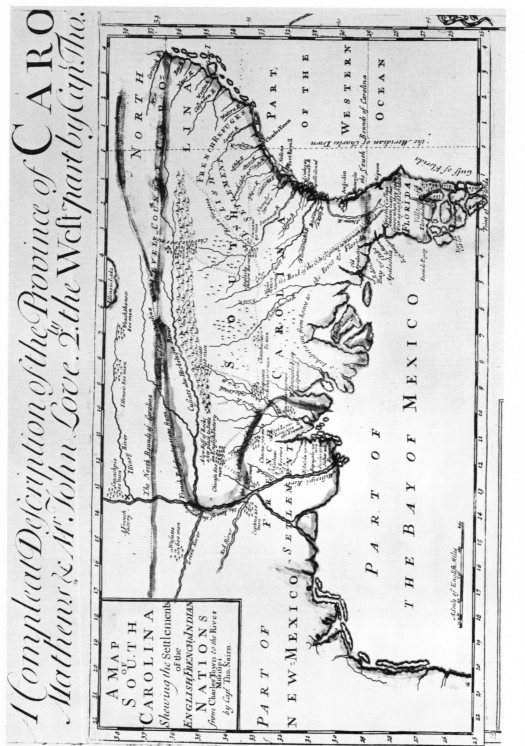

Thomas Naire, *A Map of South Carolina*. Inset from Edward Crisp, *A Compleat Description of the Province of Carolina*, 1711. The experience of Naire as an Indian agent is shown in the attention to Indian trails and villages.

Courtesy of the Library of Congress

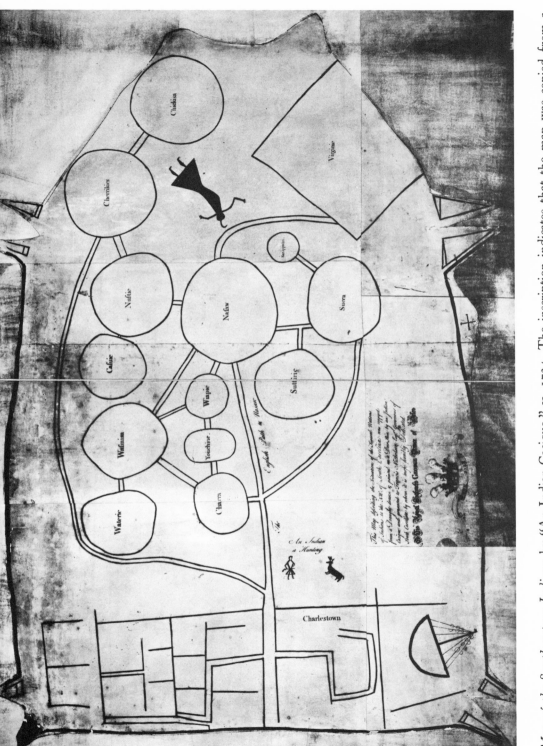

Map of the Southeastern Indians, by "An Indian Cacique," ca. 1724. The inscription indicates that the map was copied from a deerskin.

Courtesy of the Library of Congress

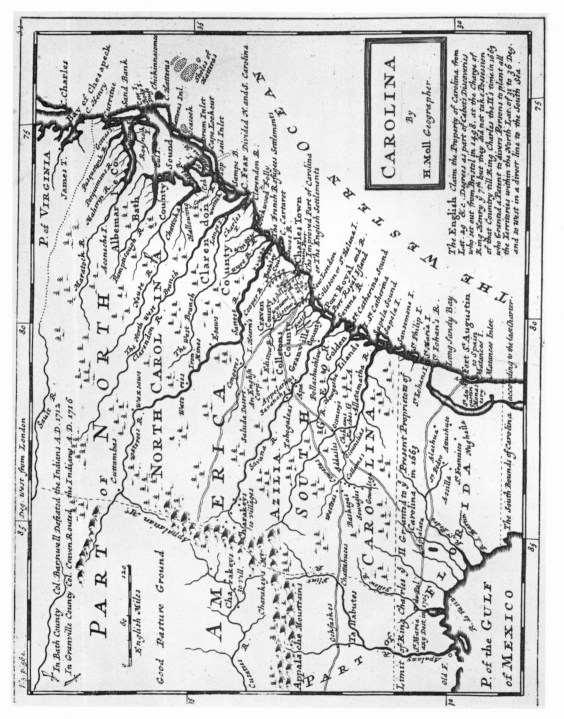

Herman Moll, *Carolina*, 1729. The many legends reveal the increasing knowledge of the Carolina back country and the Indians beyond.

Tomochichi and His Nephew, Tooanahowi. Mezzotint by John Faber after a portrait
by Willem Verelst.

Oglethorpe Presenting Tomochichi and the Indians to the Lord Trustees of the Colony of Georgia. Painting by Willem Verelst.

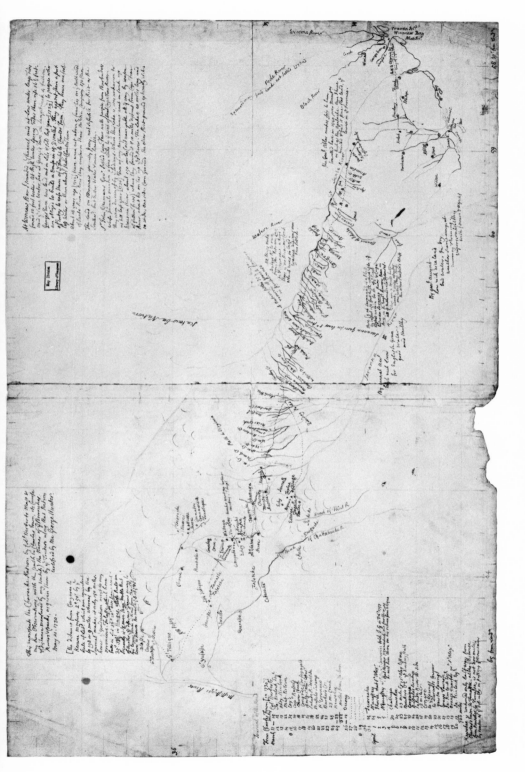

George Hunter, *Cherokee Nation and the Traders' Path*, 1730. Sir Alexander Cuming accompanied Hunter during part of the journey which is the basis of the map.
Courtesy of the Library of Congress

John Herbert and George Hunter, *A New Mapp of South Carolina*, 1744. Hunter relied heavily on the

the Chickasaws were rumormongers and troublemakers, and despite proof on one occasion to the contrary, he later repeated his accusations.[7] Chicken's 1725 trip in the Cherokee nation was brief, and as with many persons who traveled among the Indians for official reasons, he displayed little interest in the natives' life styles.

While George Chicken was working among the Cherokees on behalf of the English, Tobias Fitch was engaged in a similar mission in the Creek confederacy. Fitch evidently did not play a major role in the development of South Carolina, but he obviously was no stranger to the Indians. Arthur Middleton, president of the South Carolina Council, appointed Fitch as agent to the Creeks in 1725. He was given tasks similar to those of Commissioner Chicken. Fitch was to improve the position of the English among the Creeks by lessening the influence of the Spanish and French, which had increased since the Yamassee War. He was also to prevent the increase of hostilities between the Creeks and the Cherokees. Fitch's assignment involved many more difficulties than that of Commissioner Chicken. During the first half of the eighteenth century the Cherokees were one of the few Southern tribes that consistently supported the English, but a strong attraction to the Spanish and, to a lesser extent, the French was found among the Creeks.[8]

There were similarities between the accounts of Fitch and Chicken. Both men were essentially concerned with fulfilling their duties and neither was really interested in native culture and society. Almost all of Fitch's journal concerned his accounts of talks with the Creek leaders, their replies, observations, and rumors of Spanish activity, and reports of the extent of anti-Cherokee attitude in the confederation.

Fitch did report his reception at "Oakefusky," or Oakfuskee, a principal settlement of the Abeikas, on the Tallapoosa River in

[7] *Ibid.,* 136, 144–45, 157, 165, 172.

[8] Tobias Fitch, "Journal," in Mereness, *Travels,* 175–78 *et passim;* and Corkran, *Creek Frontier,* 71. Corkran discusses this period of Creek history which led to the development of a policy of neutrality toward the European powers. *Creek Frontier,* chap. iii. For the Anglo-Cherokee alliance, see his *Cherokee Frontier,* chap. i.

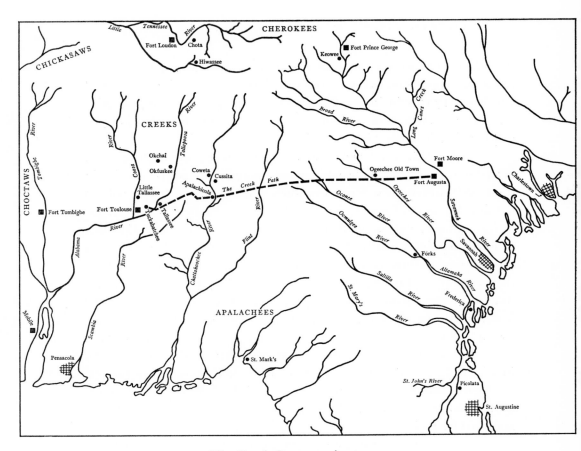

The Creek Country, circa 1700

eastern Alabama. The Abeikas were one of the subdivisions of the Upper Creeks. The Creeks were divided into the Upper Creeks, composed of Abeikas, Alabamas, and Tallapoosas, occupying some forty towns along the Coosa and Tallapoosa rivers in Alabama, and the Lower Creeks, with some twenty towns along the Ocmulgee, Flint, and Chattahoochee rivers of Georgia. Upon his arrival, July 9, 1725, he was greeted with "a great many Serimoneys." Next, he was taken to meet

all the head men of the Several Towns there about; And after passing Some Complements there was Some fowls Brought in and Set Before me;

and Befor I was Suffered to Eat the King Made the Following Speach: "I am Glad to see you here In my Town But I am Sory that I Cannot Entertain you with Such as I am Entertained when I go Down to your Great Town; But I hope you will Except of Such as I have and you are very Welcom to it."

On at least two other occasions Fitch received apologies for the amount of food offered him upon his first visit to towns, but the remarks seemingly were courtesy, not indications of an actual scarcity of food.[9]

The Englishman commented briefly on the political organization of the confederacy, but he, like Chicken, was primarily concerned with establishing pro-English leaders among the Indians. Early in his visit he sought to secure reparations from an Indian who had seriously wounded an English trader and stolen his goods and three of his Negro slaves in an attack upon the Cherokees. The accused Indian disavowed the action, but the Creek leaders, who knew of his responsibility, forced the man to promise to return part of the loot and make reparation for the remainder. Fitch seemed to doubt that the actual payment would be made. The agent's doubt was increased by his suspicions of the Creeks' professed friendship. Several times he noted in his journal his suspicions and questioned especially the intentions of one important warrior, Sepeycoffe. Sepeycoffe was the son of "Emperor" Brims of the Cowetas, who were probably the most important of the Lower Creeks. Brims, who was the single most powerful Creek during the 1720's, was not a young man, and the English naturally hoped that his successor would favor them. The Carolina agent openly criticized Sepeycoffe's pro-Spanish sentiments in September, but shortly before he left the Creeks in December, 1725, he made the warrior "Commander-in-Cheif [*sic*]" under his father. Sepeycoffe had led a raid against the Yamassees, Indian allies of the Spanish, and Fitch rewarded him with British recognition of his right to succeed his father as "emperor."[10]

[9] Fitch, "Journal," 176–77, 190.
[10] *Ibid.*, 178–84, 210–11; and Corkran, *Creek Frontier*, 71–72. On the importance of Brims and the Cowetas, see *ibid.*, 61–80.

Although Tobias Fitch achieved some success among the Creeks, especially in weakening the influence of Spain, the Muskogean confederation continued to perplex the English. Moreover, the warfare between the Creeks and the Cherokees continued unabated.

By the early autumn of 1727 the Carolina government was sufficiently alarmed to make another attempt at ending the inter-tribal conflict. In October of that year, John Herbert traveled to the Cherokee nation. Herbert had visited the Cherokees during the Yamassee War in an attempt to keep that tribe friendly to the English. The colonist continued to play a role in Indian affairs after the war and served as a joint commissioner with Chicken and William Bull in the early 1720's. In 1727 he followed Chicken as sole commissioner.[11]

Like George Chicken and Tobias Fitch, John Herbert was primarily concerned with the success of his mission. His preoccupation was reflected in his journal, which was brief with short, irregular entries. After arriving at Keowee in early November, 1727, he began four months of almost constant travel among the Lower and Middle Cherokee settlements. Everywhere he went, the commissioner inspected licenses of traders for irregularities, expressed his concern at the traders' granting of credit to the natives, and held conferences with the Cherokee chiefs.[12]

Probably because of the pressure of official duties and perhaps because of a lack of interest in native culture, John Herbert made no observations of Indian civilization. His journal did reveal the fatigue and frustrations faced by some British officials while traveling among the Southern Indians.

In 1728 the Creeks were forced to break with the Yamassees and the Spanish. War parties of Upper Creeks, who were far more pro-British than the Lower Creeks, raided the Yamassees, and in December of that year a Carolina expedition destroyed the Yamassee settlements near St. Augustine. Convinced that the Spanish could offer

[11] *Journal of Colonel John Herbert, Commissioner of Indian Affairs for the Province of South Carolina*, ed. Alexander S. Salley, 3; and Corkran, *Creek Frontier*, 75–78.

[12] Herbert, *Journal*, 10–12, 18–19 *et passim*.

them no real protection, the Lower Creeks joined their Upper brethren and made peace with the English. The Creek-Cherokee war continued, but with less intensity.

Sir Alexander Cuming, the next traveler of note among the Southern Indians, did not comment upon the Indian situation in the Southeast, but he probably realized the need for strengthening the ties with the Cherokees in the event that the new Anglo-Creek alliance should prove short-lived. Cuming, second baronet Culter, Aberdeenshire, was born about 1690. In 1714 he was admitted to the Scottish bar, and in 1720 he was elected a fellow of the Royal Society. In December, 1729, the baronet arrived in Charles-Town, South Carolina. The reasons for his trip to America and his short visit among the Cherokees during the next year have been matters of conjecture. Nearly all information about Cuming's trips comes, not directly from him, but from contemporary London newspapers. The relatively brief accounts were primarily a log of his travels and observations about the novel natives of the New World.[13]

Speculations about the reasons for Cuming's tour are varied. According to one story, he left home because his wife dreamed he should visit the Cherokee country. A more plausible explanation involves his scientific interest. He had an interest in the products and minerals of America and might have come to collect valuable mineral samples and New World flora and fauna. The Cherokee journey has also been the subject of speculation. Cuming may have been acting in some official capacity, but the excursion may have been merely the result of a natural Scottish curiosity.

Another possible explanation for the trip involves the baronet's financial plight. Cuming owed the sum of £1500 to various Carolinians, and even after his return to England his financial problems continued. From 1737 to 1765 he was confined to Fleet prison as a

[13] Sir Alexander Cuming, "Account of the Cherokee Indians and of Sir Alexander Cuming's Journey amongst Them"; "Some Heads of Sir Alexander Cuming's Journey to the Cherokee Mountains," in Samuel C. Williams, ed., *Early Travels in the Tennessee Country, 1540–1800*, 122–38. Reprinted from the London newspapers *Daily Journal, Daily Courant,* and *Daily Post,* June–October, 1730.

debtor and lived the last ten years of his life as a poor brother of Charterhouse. The Scotsman hoped to improve his finances through some scheme involving the Indians and their lands. At one point during his journey he noted the discovery of "some Iron Stone." In England he sought recognition as overlord of the Cherokees, a claim rejected by the Board of Trade. He also proposed the settling of several millions of Jews in the Cherokee country. The colonization plan was also rejected, despite the claim that it would greatly reduce the national debt. Cuming also proposed unacceptable plans for reforming colonial currency and banking. For a man who spent much of his life devising monetary projects, the hope of material gain from a visit with the Indians did not seem unreasonable. The only reason stated by Cuming for the 1730 sojourn was a desire to explore the mountains after discovering iron, even though he was already traveling west when he recorded the discovery.[14]

On March 13, 1730, Cuming left a plantation near Charles-Town, where he had probably been a guest, and set off for Fort Congaree, near present-day Columbia. He was accompanied by George Chicken, the former Commissioner of Indian Affairs, and George Hunter, a surveyor who was working on a new map of Cherokee territory. Chicken and Hunter traveled too slowly for Cuming, and he left them at Congaree and hurried westward. By March 23 he was at Keowee, where he employed Ludovick Grant as guide. Many years later Grant recalled his strange employer and his unusual haste. He remembered that the Scotsman never stayed more than one night in one place and often remained only a few hours at each settlement.[15]

[14] Cuming, "Some Heads," 130–31; Alexander Hewatt, *Historical Account of the Rise and Progress of the Colonies of South Carolina and Georgia,* II, 3–11; and Samuel G. Drake, "Early History of Georgia and Sir Alexander Cuming's Embassy to the Cherokee," *New England Historical and Genealogical Register,* Vol. XXVI (July, 1872), 360–71.

[15] Cuming, "Some Heads," 129–34. In the mid-1750's Grant gave a deposition of his opinion of a possible land cession during Cuming's trip. Concerned primarily with refuting that idea, it contains little useful material for assessing Cuming and his trip, but it is one of the few colonial notices of the Scotsman. It has been printed as "Historical Relation of Facts Delivered by Ludovick Grant, Indian Trader, to His Excellency the Governor of

Because of the hurried, brief nature of his visit, it was natural that Cuming usually commented only on the dramatic aspects of Cherokee life. Frequently the observations indicated little of the writer's reactions and were equally sparse in descriptive information. For example, on one occasion the Scotsman noted the presence of scalps in a village, but unlike other travelers he did not reveal his opinion of native warfare. At another time, he sought to secure some mysterious herbs and roots from the Indians, but their purpose and description were omitted from his journal.[16]

His only extensive commentary on native customs dealt with political authority and its trappings. At the beginning of the account, Cuming included a discussion of the political organization of the Cherokee nation. According to him, there were seven "Mother Towns" in the "Nation." These were "Tannassie, Kettoah, Ustenary, Telliquo, Estootowie, Keyowee, [and] Noyohee." Each of the towns had a "King . . . elected out of certain Families, and they regard only the Descent by the Mother's Sides." Cuming omitted Chota of the Overhill portion of the nation, which was actually the true "Mother Town." The "Mother Town" of "Telliquo" had not only a "King," but also two "Princes." Other towns had only a single "Prince." Cuming believed that the "King" was more of a "Civil Magistrate" than an actual ruler and that the "Head Warrior" of each settlement possessed the most authority. "Conjurers" were also deemed unusually important in native government. Finally, the adventurer stated that in 1730 the highest authority was held by Moytoy of "Telliquo," or Tellico, who "presides at present as Emperor over the whole [nation]." Because, during the course of his tour, Cuming crowned Moytoy "emperor" of all the Cherokees, it was not readily apparent from the account whether or not the traveler believed the title to be of native origin; but he did assert that Moytoy had "absolute unlimited power." In reality, Moytoy did not have the greatest pres-

South Carolina," *South Carolina Historical and Genealogical Magazine*, Vol. X (Jan., 1909), 54–68.

[16] Cuming, "Some Heads," 135, 137.

tige, at least not before English intervention. The "Uku," or First Beloved Man, of Chota had that honor.[17]

Cuming's interest in political organization was natural, since his greatest concern was the securing from the Cherokees a formal acknowledgment of loyalty and even subordination to the British monarchy. He evidently succeeded in achieving this goal because of naïve brashness, charisma, and a large amount of good fortune. Even before he encountered his first Cherokee, he may have realized his strange ability to influence the Indians. At Congaree, a "Catarba" [Catawba] chief, "Captain Haw," wished to honor Cuming. According to the writer, the Indian wanted to "salute him with Feathers, . . . dance around him during the whole Night, and would make him a Present of all their Skins." The weary traveler declined because the ceremony would have been too noisy. Later, he arrived at a Cherokee town during a violent thunderstorm. A native "Conjurer" associated the storm with Cuming's appearance and informed him "that he [the native] knew that he was come amongst them to rule and that their whole Nation must do whatever he bid them."[18]

The fact that Cuming had already demanded and secured compliance with his wishes may have influenced the Cherokee medicine man. Immediately upon his arrival at Keowee, the visitor revealed his strong desire to secure a definite pledge of loyalty from the Cherokees. The British traders at the town strongly advised against using any force, but in a bold move Cuming achieved his purpose. Assembling the village leaders, he violated native protocol on two counts. He did not seek to persuade but instead demanded that the Cherokees toast the British monarch, and he was armed during the meeting. Both his bellicose attitude and his wearing of weapons at such a gathering were serious breaches of native custom, but the Indians were awed or cowed into submission. Cuming related the episode in the third person: "arm'd with three Cases of Pistols, a Gun, and his Sword; [he entered] where the head Men of the Town, in the midst of 300, own'd

[17] Cuming, "Account," 122–23, and Corkran, *Cherokee Frontier*, 3–16.
[18] Cuming, "Some Heads," 131–33.

Obedience to him on their Knees." Whether by luck or intuitive under-standing of the Indian's respect for courage, Sir Alexander Cuming had gained what he believed to be loyalty and submission to Great Britain. Ludovick Grant later thought the gesture to be merely a toast, but he and the other traders were amazed at the control the Scotsman seemed to exercise over the Indians. Nonchalantly, Cuming departed on the brief tour of the nation, during which he was wel-comed with more ceremony and obedience.[19]

The climax of the tour came at Nequasse, a Middle Cherokee town, on April 3. There, among dignitaries from throughout the nation, Moytoy who was probably Head Warrior of the Overhill Cherokees, was crowned "emperor" of his people. During the cere-mony, Cuming was "stroked with 13 Eagle Tails," and the people danced and chanted all day while fasting "as their Custom is on solemn Occasions." The crown of the chief of Nequasse was given to Cuming as a token of loyalty. Cuming provided no description of the crown, but Grant remembered it as a red or yellow cap made of opossum fur.[20]

At some point during his travels, Cuming decided to take some Cherokees to England, and after the installation of Moytoy, Cuming started for the coast accompanied by six red men. On April 13, a month and nearly one thousand miles after his departure, Cuming ar-rived at Charles-Town. On May 13, he, seven Indians—another native had joined the party—and Eleazer Wiggan departed for Lon-don. Wiggan, affectionately known as "Old Rabbit" by the Cherokees, was one of the earliest known traders among the Cherokees and served as interpreter for the group. In Great Britain the Indians proved to be quite a sensation. They met King George II, presented him with the Nequasse crown, and signed a treaty of friendship and commerce. Despite the honor bestowed upon him by the Cherokees and the bene-fits to Great Britain from his travels, Cuming seemingly was not well received at home. Only upon the insistence of the Cherokees was he

[19] *Ibid.*, 133, 135; Cuming, "Account," 124–25; and Grant, "Relation," 55ff.
[20] *Ibid.*; Cuming, "Account," 125–26; and Cuming, "Some Heads," 136.

present at the signing of the treaty, and the British officials would have nothing to do with any of his schemes for reaping profits from his New World adventure. The natives arrived back at Charles-Town in mid-November, 1730, having provided diversion for the British and stimulated interest in the colonies, which probably aided the proposed colony of Georgia then under discussion.[21]

The importance of Sir Alexander Cuming in white-Indian relations, indeed his whole presence in America, is not clear. Evidently he was not forgotten by the Cherokees. Fifteen years after his visit, the Indians still venerated the 1730 treaty that he had indirectly fostered. In 1745, a large group of Cherokees welcomed a new governor to South Carolina. Along with the speeches of greeting and assertions of friendship, James Glen, the new governor, was shown a copy of the document signed in London.[22]

The Cherokees had long been allies of the English when Sir Alexander Cuming suddenly appeared among them, but the trip of the extraordinary Scotsman no doubt added to the strength of the Anglo-Cherokee alliance. As the 1730's drew to a close the need for such friendship was apparent to the English. War with Spain became an increasing possibility, and in 1739 James Oglethorpe, leader of the colony which added to the New World tensions, undertook a western journey for the purpose of making a firm alliance with the Creeks, Choctaws, and Chickasaws, all of whom were being eagerly courted by the Spanish and the French. He was accompanied by a party of rangers or frontiersmen, one of whom left a short account of the native society encountered on the trip.

Despite the official nature of the journey, the "Ranger," unlike Chicken, Fitch, Herbert, and Cuming, was almost entirely concerned with the ordinary aspects of his travels and of Indian life. On July 8, 1739, the man left Frederica, Georgia, in a party of about twenty-five whites and "some Indians all well Armed." The Indians provided an

---

[21] *Ibid.*, 136–37, "Treaty of 'Friendship and Commerce,' " in Williams, *Early Travels*, 138–43.

[22] Corkran, *Cherokee Frontier*, 13.

abundance of venison, turkey, and buffalo meat, as well as wild honey. On August 7, as the party approached the Lower Creek town of "Couettaus," or Coweta, the travelers found "Cakes and Bags of Flower [flour] etca. which the Indians had hung up in Trees for our Refreshmt." On the next day, camp was made only a few miles from Coweta, and the natives sent a variety of food to the site. Lack of food was obviously not a problem.[23]

At noon on August 8, the Englishmen entered the town and were greeted by the "King and some of their Cheifs [*sic*]." After the hosts had provided logs covered with bear skins as resting places, the ceremonial "Black Drink" was served. The anonymous writer recorded the ritual:

The head Warriours of the Indians brought us black Drink in Conkshells which they presented to us and as we were drinking they kept Hooping and Hallowing as a Token of gladness in seeing us. This Drink is made of a Leaf called by the English Casena (and much Resembles the Leaf of Bohea Tea) It is very Plenty in this Country.

After dining with the Creek headmen, the visitors were honored with a dance. The writer was most impressed by the appearance of the performers. He described their dress as "very wild and frightfull" and noted the multi-colored paints used on the faces and the custom of cutting the hair except for "three Locks one of wch hangs over their Forehead like a horses fore Top." He must have been describing the mens' hair style, because he praised the women's care of their extremely long hair. The scantily clad women who were "mostly naked to the Waist" also drew his comments. Finally, he remarked on the rattles and "Balls" attached to the dancers' bodies and the unusual movements of the performers.[24]

The common elements of Creek life were also briefly noted. The "Ranger" indicated that houses were built of "Stakes and plaistered with Clay Mixed with Moss which makes them very warm

[23] "A Ranger's Report of Travels with General Oglethorpe, 1739–1742," in Mereness, *Travels,* 218–20.
[24] *Ibid.,* 220–21.

and Tite." Food was prepared in large pottery pans. Corn was ground in wooden mortars made from tree trunks and afterwards poured through a cane or reed sieve to remove the husks. The division of labor between the sexes was also noticed: women took care of the home and worked in the fields, while the men hunted a wide variety of animals and fowls. The dependence of the Creeks on European traders was indirectly reported by the traveler. He wrote that animal skins and furs were sold "to the Traders for Powder [,] Ball and what other Necessaries they want."

On August 12 the English party moved to nearby Cussita, and for two weeks Oglethorpe held conferences with the Indians. He especially worked to settle any conflicts and disagreements that the natives might have had with the English traders. The Indians amused their guests with more dances, and on at least one occasion some of the English joined the antics, much to the natives' delight. The Oglethorpe party departed after distributing gifts and renewing old treaties of friendship with the Creek confederacy and Choctaw and Chickasaw delegates who attended the conference. The "Ranger" did not comment on the treaties or on the tribes that met with Oglethorpe.

At Augusta on September 13, word reached the expedition that war with Spain had been declared. The anonymous "Ranger" served with General Oglethorpe in his campaigns against the Spanish in Florida in 1740, and then he disappeared from written history.[25]

Between 1720 and 1740 George Chicken, Tobias Fitch, John Herbert, Sir Alexander Cuming, and a "Ranger" wrote brief accounts of their travels among the Creeks and the Cherokees. Except for Cuming, the men were on official missions. Chicken, Fitch, and Herbert were almost entirely concerned with the relationship of the Indians with the British colonists in the South. Occasionally comments were made on some aspect of native culture, but these were casual and usually related to the writers' preoccupation.

The Scottish baronet and the unknown frontiersman were the most interesting of these travelers. Despite the limited amount of in-

[25] *Ibid.*, 221–36; and Corkran, *Creek Frontier*, 101.

formation regarding Cuming's hasty journey, he left a valuable account of the Cherokees. He was mistaken in some instances about Indian political organization, but the natives' reaction to the nobleman's impetuosity and impudence provides insight into their culture. The "Ranger" was concerned solely with the everyday life of the Lower Creeks. The details of clothing, food, and houses are useful in understanding Indian technology. The rarity of accounts by members of the lower or middle socio-economic class in colonial America increases the importance of his journal.

In the two decades after 1740, British travelers continued to visit the Southern Indians. A Presbyterian minister left a lengthy account of his efforts to convert the Cherokees, an Anglican clergyman wrote of the sad remnant of a Tidewater tribe, and the young George Washington was thrilled by a native dance.

IX

*Travelers Among the Southern
Indians, 1740–1760*

URING the 1740's many of the British colonists in North America and their brethren across the Atlantic were primarily occupied with fighting the Spanish and the French. Yet, few campaigns of real importance were waged in the Southeast during King George's War. Most of the fighting consisted of relatively small expeditions like those led by General James Oglethorpe against St. Augustine in 1740 and in 1743. Between British attacks, the Spanish attempted the capture of Frederica, Georgia, as a step toward their major goals of taking Savannah and Charles-Town. Both the British and the Spanish failed in their objectives, and after Oglethorpe's 1743 campaign, the colonies and their mother countries turned their attention to the European and New England theaters of war.[1] During the war there was continued English contact with the Southeastern Indians, but perhaps because of the warfare the number of known travelers was not large. Three men did visit the Southern Indians for very different reasons.

The score of years which followed the Treaty of Aix-la-

---

[1] For the Southern colonies during the war see Corkran, *Cherokee Frontier*, chap. i; Corkran, *Creek Frontier*, chaps. v and vi; and Norman W. Caldwell, "The Southern Frontier during King George's War," *Journal of Southern History*, Vol. VII (Feb., 1941), 37–54.

Chapelle of 1748 was not tranquil in the history of Anglo-Indian relations in the South. The old hatred between the Creek confederacy and the Cherokee nation became bitter fighting between 1750 and 1752. The English generally supported the Cherokees, but many members of both the confederacy and the nation emerged from the conflict displeased with the British colonists. However, the essential concern of these colonists was to prevent the Spanish and French from benefiting from the fighting and to maintain commercial ties with both tribes.[2] The turbulence in the Southern wilderness did not prevent white settlers from moving westward or gentlemen speculators from attempting to profit from the expansion. One of the first tasks of a speculator was to survey his vast tract and divide it into small plots for eventual sale to frontiersmen or for renting to tenants. During one such surveying expedition a young Virginian, at the time unknown except to friends and relatives, but destined for world fame, encountered the native Americans.[3]

On March 11, 1748, the sixteen-year-old George Washington left Mount Vernon, at that time the home of Lawrence Washington, his half-brother, and joined George William Fairfax to begin a trip over the Blue Ridge. Fairfax, who was to become Washington's life-long friend, was seven years older, and during the journey the young lad consistently referred to him as "Mr. Fairfax" or "George Fairfax." After one day's travel they met James Genn, an experienced surveyor who was in charge of the party, at George Neville's inn. The ultimate destination of the expedition was a wilderness tract on the South Branch of the Potomac River, a minor portion of the great domain of Thomas, sixth earl of Fairfax, who was proprietor of the Northern Neck during the late colonial period. George William Fairfax was to act as representative for his kinsman, and Washington,

---

[2] Corkran, *Creek Frontier*, chaps. vi–xiv; and Corkran, *Cherokee Frontier*, chaps. iii–ix.

[3] On the expansion of the Southern colonies, see Robert L. Meriwether, *Expansion of South Carolina, 1729–1765*; Thomas P. Abernethy, *Three Virginia Frontiers*, chap. ii; and Douglas S. Freeman, *George Washington, a Biography*, I, chaps. v–vi.

who had learned the rudiments of surveying, hoped to gain further experience by working with Genn.[4]

Enroute to their destination the members of the party spent three days marking off some land owned by young Fairfax. On March 17, the small band of Virginians left Frederick Town on the final stage of the journey to the South Branch. Genn did not take a direct route to the tract, which was west of the frontier settlement, but instead turned north into Maryland for a short distance and then recrossed into Virginia and followed the river south. The party reached the home of Thomas Cresap near the junction of the north and south branches of the Potomac on March 21.

Rains, which had hampered the Englishmen throughout the journey, caused a three-day delay at Cresap's, but the monotony of waiting was broken on the second day by the appearance of approximately thirty Indians whose tribe was not identified. Young Washington was delighted at the sight of the natives, who were members of a war party returning home "with only one Scalp." After being liberally plied with alcohol, the Indians performed a dance. In his diary the lad recorded his vivid impressions of the encounter. He wrote:

There manner of Daucing is as follows Viz They clear a Large Circle and make a Great Fire in y. middle then seats themselves around it y. Speaker makes a grand speech telling them in what Manner they are to Daunce after he has finished y. best Dauncer jumps up as one awaked out of a Sleep and runs and Jumps about y. Ring in a most comical Manner he is followed by y. Rest then begins there Musicians to Play ye. Musick is a Pot half [full] of Water with a Deerskin streched over it as tight as it can and a goard with some Shott in it to Rattle and a Piece of an horses Tail tied to it to make it look fine y. one keeps Rattling and y. other Drumming all y. while y. others is Dauncing.

The young Tidewater gentleman also spent the following day with the Indians, but despite his initial interest he tersely noted in his

[4] George Washington, *Diaries of George Washington, 1748–1799*, ed. John C. Fitzpatrick, I, 3–4. The best account of the 1748 journey of Washington is in the masterful study by Freeman, *Washington*, I, 202–23.

journal that "nothing Remarkable on thursday but only being with y. Indians all day so shall slip [skip?] it."[5]

The brief encounter with the war party was evidently George Washington's only peaceful contact with Southern Indians during the colonial period. After less than two weeks of surveying, he and young Fairfax returned home. As with many other travelers, he was greatly impressed with the novel dances of the natives, but because of a lack of time or interest he did not record his impressions of other native characteristics.

At the end of the 1750's two British travelers contacted very diverse groups of native Americans. One of these men was Andrew Burnaby. The major British interest in the natives lay with the important tribes to the west, but an occasional traveler still recorded his impressions of the pacified remnants of the coastal tribes, and Burnaby was one such visitor. In the spring of 1759 Burnaby, the eldest son of a wealthy Anglican clergyman and a minister himself, arrived in Virginia from Spithead, England. For six months he traveled through the colonies north of the Old Dominion. From Williamsburg he went to Winchester, Virginia, and on to Newport, Boston, and Portsmouth, New Hampshire, where he sailed for home.[6]

During the course of his tour the clergyman visited the "Pamunky Indian town" in King William County, Virginia. The Pamunky (or Pamunkey) Indians were an important tribe within the Powhatan confederation when the English arrived in 1607. In the 150 years since European settlement the tribe had largely disappeared, and by 1759 revealed little if any of their former glory. They were probably the only Indian tribe located in the Old Dominion at the time of Burnaby's visit. In a terse remark that characterized his journal, Burnaby indicated that in his opinion the Indians had declined in numbers and importance because of "intemperance and disease." He did not elaborate on the nature of the "intemperances" or the source of the diseases. In other comments he noted that the

[5] Washington, *Diaries,* I, 4–7.
[6] *Travels through the Middle Settlements in North America,* 4.

Indians lived in "little wigwams or cabins" and wore European clothing. In addition to being dependent upon the English for their clothing, the Indians also earned their livelihood by hunting and fishing for the Virginians.[7]

All of Burnaby's observations on the English colonies were short, and those dealing with the Pamunky band of Indians were extremely brief. His journal did indicate that an interest in native Americans, even the sad remnant of a once proud tribe, continued to exist among European travelers along the Atlantic coast.

An important travel account of the Cherokee nation was recorded during the turbulent period. A Presbyterian missionary, the Reverend Mr. William Richardson, journeyed to the Cherokee country immediately before the outbreak of the Cherokee War in 1760. He also briefly contacted the Catawba tribe in South Carolina on his trip west. The missionary was naturally concerned with Cherokee religious life, but his journal also contained information on other aspects of Indian civilization and recorded the growing tension between the natives and the English.

In the 1750's the Presbyterian church in the Southern colonies became interested in missionary activity among the Indians. The Society for Managing the Mission and Schools among the Indians was organized, and the Society for the Propagation of the Gospel of Scotland (Presbyterian) provided some financial support. Late in 1757 the Reverend Mr. John Martin became the first Presbyterian missionary to the Southern Indians. At least by early 1758 he was among the Overhill Cherokees. For reasons that are not definitely known, but probably because of illness and discouragement, Martin remained with the natives for less than a year. Richardson was chosen to continue the work.[8]

---

[7] Burnaby, *Travels*, 30; Hodge, *Handbook of American Indians*, II, 197–99; and Brown, *Catawba Indians*, 3.

[8] Samuel C. Williams, "An Account of the Presbyterian Mission to the Cherokees, 1751–1759," *Tennessee Historical Magazine*, 2nd ser., Vol. I (Jan., 1931), 125–29. For some reason the Presbyterian church's efforts among the Cherokees during the colonial period have been overlooked by certain writers. Brown credits the Anglican Society for the

William Richardson was born in England in 1729. At the age of twenty-one he graduated from the University of Glasgow and in the same year sailed for America. After living and studying for several years with the Reverend Dr. Samuel Davies he was ordained as an Indian missionary in July, 1758. Davies, who was the leader of the Presbyterian church in Virginia and a major force behind the organization of the Indian mission, and George Webb, another member of the Presbyterian Indian Society, accompanied Richardson to Williamsburg to solicit the support of Governor Francis Fauquier. The royal governor expressed interest in the project and supplied letters of introduction to several of the English officials in the Cherokee nation.[9]

On October 5, 1758, Richardson left Williamsburg and began a slow journey across the western portions of Virginia and the Carolinas. He paused frequently to preach and to visit friends and was further delayed by rumors of Cherokee hostility toward the English. He was also awaiting the arrival of an interpreter. Either to fill the idle time or by previous intent, the minister visited the Catawba Indians. By the mid-eighteenth century the Catawbas were a small

Propagation of the Gospel in Foreign Parts with supporting Richardson. *Catawba Indians*, 248. Woodward credits Gideon Blackburn, who worked with the Cherokees during the early nineteenth century, with being the "first Presbyterian missionary to the Cherokees." *Cherokees*, 123–27, 130, and inscription beneath engraving of Blackburn.

[9] William Richardson, "An Account of my Proceedings since I Accepted the Indian Mission in October 2d, 1758," New York Public Library, Wilberforce Eames Collection, Manuscript Division, Oct. 2–5, 1758; and Williams, "Account of the Presbyterian Mission," 127–29. The "Account," which is actually a diary, will be cited as Richardson, "Diary." Williams, who did a real service in bringing to public attention one of the few accounts of colonial missionary activity in the South, did poor editing and often misread the material. For example, Williams' entry of January 9, 1759, indicated that the missionary rented an Indian cabin for "100 shillings Virginia money" for a four-month period, but the diary reads "18 teen shillings." The difference reveals a considerable variation in the value placed by the Indians on their homes. Of even more importance is the error in the entry of December 29, 1758. Richardson had some trouble with a young man and, according to Williams, remarked, "The Saucy fellow was a white man who in general are worse than others . . . ." The diary actually reads "The Saucy fellow was a white man's . . . ." Instead of the minister criticizing the English traders, almost certainly he was referring to the offspring of English-Indian marriages. It might also be noted that the entire diary, which began on October 2, 1758, and ended on March 14, 1759, is more than twice the length of the portion printed by Williams.

tribe, having declined greatly after the Yamassee War. They were never a nation in the sense that other Indian groups were, and by this time they included remnants of several Tidewater and Piedmont tribes, especially those of the Siouan language family. At the time of Richardson's visit they lived in western South Carolina. He was momentarily delayed because of rumors of a contagious disease among the Catawbas, but on November 8 he and a Mr. McCorkle went to Cheraw Town. At the village the English traveler met a Saponi Indian, Captain Harry, who knew some English. Captain Harry was not willing to discuss religion with the minister, but he did tell the visitor that "old Indian make no Sabbath & young Indian make no Sabbath." Richardson also learned that, at least among these Indians, persons of his profession were known as "Sunday Men."[10]

Leaving the Cheraw Town, which he noted as being constructed in a circular fashion, the missionary went to visit King Heigler, who was perhaps the greatest of Catawba leaders. Although the "Sunday Man" later learned that King Heigler could speak some English, on this occasion he was forced to converse with the chief through his son-in-law. The Presbyterian sought to convince the two Indians that man did not "die like the Dogs," as they believed, and that "some thing different" from the body lived after death. The minister seemingly inquired into the possibility of doing missionary work among the Catawbas, and King Heigler did not refuse, but he indicated that the time was not right. It was the hunting season, and the people were busy. After promising the old man some corn if he would come to the home of a Captain Simpson, Richardson returned to Cheraw Town. Once more at the village, the missionary talked with another Indian, Cheraw George, evidently a leader of the town. Besides telling him of "God, our obligation to know & to do his will," the Scotsman asked Cheraw George if schools might be established. The native was not enthusiastic, because other "Sunday Men" had made similar requests and then left, never to return. He was, however,

<hr>

[10] Richardson, "Diary," Nov. 7–8, 1758; and Brown, *Catawba Indians*, chaps. i, vii, and viii.

willing to abide by the decision of King Heigler. At the close of the busy day, Richardson returned to McCorkle's and on the next day traveled to Captain Simpson's home. On November 11, 1758, King Heigler appeared at the captain's, and he and the minister talked "a good deal." Richardson found that "when the Discourse was about corn . . . he seemed to understand, but anything else he seemed at a Loss." "He talks a little English," the white concluded. Upon receiving ten shillings to buy corn, King Heigler left to go hunting. After remaining with Captain Simpson for four days, the missionary continued on his journey.[11]

Three days after leaving Simpson's, Richardson met Martin, who was returning from visiting the Cherokees, at Ninety Six, a frontier settlement between Congaree and the Lower Cherokee villages. Martin relieved the new missionary's fears of an Indian uprising and informed him that there was no need for haste because many of the Cherokees were on their annual autumn hunting expeditions. Richardson declined an invitation to travel with Martin to Charles-Town from whence both might journey to the Cherokees. Instead, it was decided that Martin should return to Virginia and seek greater financial support for the mission while Richardson continued west. In the company of some other Englishmen, Richardson left Ninety Six and reached Fort Prince George on November 29. The fort, which had been constructed by South Carolina in 1753, was located on the Keowee River, opposite the Lower Cherokee town of Keowee.

The next day was Sunday, and while the others rested, Richardson preached to a gathering of Cherokees. On Monday the travelers continued their journey. They were in haste because snow storms might close the mountain passes at any time. The storms did not materialize, but the trip was not easy. The road was poor, and on some days a "very hard Frost" added to the difficulties. On December 15 the missionary arrived at Fort Loudoun, having traveled, according to

---

[11] Richardson, "Diary," Nov. 8–14, 1758. On King Heigler or Hagler, see Brown, *Catawba Indians*, 230–51 *et passim*.

his calculations, 760 miles since leaving Williamsburg.[12] Fort Loudoun, which was to be his headquarters for nearly a month, had been built by the South Carolina and Virginia governments during 1756 and 1757. Located at the junction of the Tellico and Little Tennessee rivers and near the Overhill Cherokee "capital" of Chota, the fort was designed to protect the Overhills from the French and Indian enemies and to maintain English influence among the Overhill Cherokees. Fort Prince George was to serve a similar function among the Lower Cherokees.

The major interest of William Richardson was naturally his missionary work, and he knew enough of Indian civilization to seek official native sanction for his efforts. Three days after his arrival at the fort he went to see Connecorte, better known to the English as Old Hop. Old Hop was Uku or Fire King of Chota, Emperor of the Cherokees and the most powerful individual among the Cherokee Nation in 1758. Old Hop, who was old and lame, greeted the minister and his guide, one Ensign Boggs, in his sweat house. The emperor seemed pleased at the coming of the missionary, but he delayed granting permission for the minister to preach until a council could be held. Richardson was content for the time being, because his interpreter had not arrived.[13]

While the missionary waited for his interpreter and permission to perform publicly his duties, he preached to the Fort Loudoun soldiers and sought to learn more about his intended congregation. He visited the towns near the fort and privately discussed religion, both Christian and native, with the Indians. The interpreter arrived early in January, but permission to preach was not forthcoming. The "head men" informed Richardson that they were too concerned with recent injuries to a party of Cherokees in Virginia to act upon his request, but the Presbyterian realized that they were not really interested in mis-

[12] Richardson, "Diary," Nov. 17–Dec. 17 [15], 1758. The mistake in recording the date is one of few such errors.

[13] *Ibid.*, Dec. 18, 1758. The "emperorship" was of English, not native, origin. On Old Hop, see Corkran, *Cherokee Frontier*, 16, 42 *et passim*, and John R. Alden, *John Stuart and the Southern Colonial Frontier, 1754–1775*, 45, 64 *et passim*.

sionary activity. He was, however, invited to move to "Chote" (Chota), where it would be more convenient for him to converse with the natives. Permission to preach never came, but while he waited at Chota, Richardson tried to gain the native leaders' favor. He frequently entertained Old Hop's son, Standing Turkey, who was to succeed his father as emperor, and Oconostota, Great Warrior of the Cherokees, but within two weeks realized that his salary was not sufficient to feed the many Indians who called on him and expected to be fed. He also gave gifts of clothing to Old Hop, Standing Turkey, and the Great Warrior. Food, gifts, and entreaties were to no avail, and in the same entry that complained of the cost of feeding the Cherokees, the minister made his first mention of leaving the nation. Two weeks later he did leave the Overhills. On February 6, 1759, the missionary and his interpreter began a rapid journey to Fort Prince George. Despite mountain snow, cold rains (which caused a day's delay), tired horses, and illness, the two men reached the fort after eight days, half the time of the December journey.[14]

The Presbyterian missionary worked among the Lower Cherokees for three weeks. The Indians were, if anything, even more disinterested in his efforts. On one occasion, a native leader informed the Scotsman that "he had told his y[oun]g Peo: to take good Notice of my Talk, & while I was talking to him fell asleep alas what little acct. do they make of such Things, poor Encouragement." Wawhatchee, First Warrior of the Lower Cherokees, suggested that Richardson gain the support of the warriors with gifts, or else they would turn the minister's words to "ridicule." As for himself, the First Warrior had "heard eno[ugh] of these Things [Christianity] already." Animosity toward the English continued to increase, and on March 5 the white traveler left the Cherokee nation. In two days of hard travel, which exhausted both man and beast, he reached Ninety Six.[15]

During his stay among the Cherokees, William Richardson commented on a variety of items within the Indians' society and cul-

---

[14] Richardson, "Diary," Dec. 19, 1758–Feb. 14, 1759.
[15] *Ibid.*, Feb. 15–Mar. 7, 1759.

ture. Many of the observations were indirectly brought into the journal. For example, the traveler complained of having to feed too many Indians but noted that such generosity was the native custom. Once, Richardson refused Standing Turkey's request for clothing but realized that the man had given away part of his costume. The missionary also learned that Indian children were not corrected by corporal punishment but were doused with water or given a "Physick wc [which] does as well," in the opinion of the Cherokees. The visitor wanted to educate the young people, but the Indians feared that they would be whipped for misbehavior. Despite assurance by the white man that rods would not be used, the natives departed without indicating any desire to have the boys and girls educated.[16]

The Presbyterian revealed some interest in life within the Cherokee villages. On his first visit to Old Hop he commented that the old man's sweat house was "built like a cone" and was "very warm." He also provided a good description of the Chota Town House. He wrote:

Their Town houses are built in the Form of Sugar Loaf & will hold 4 or 500 Peo: they are supported by ten Pillars at the Foot of most of them are seats for the great Men among them, on yr right hand where in, sets on these Seats first, The Treasurer, on the 2d Hop, on the 3d, the Prince of ye Former Year, on the 4th The chief Beloved Man of the present Year wm they call Prince, in the 6 the Head Warrior &c.

The missionary also stated that the building was used for relaxation; there the men talked and smoked and occasionally slept. Dances were held in the Town House, and the white witnessed a dance at Chota. He reported that he

went to their Town-house where a great many were met & were dancing round a Cane Fire going from West to East, their young Peo: seemed very

---

[16] *Ibid.*, Jan. 23, 30, 1759. The January 23 passage is one of the most garbled in Williams' edition. Richardson's assurance that the children would not be punished was omitted. It also appeared from the reading of the printed text that the missionary gave a shirt to the Great Warrior in hopes of securing permission to preach publicly. He actually gave the garment to Old Hop. Neither omission was indicated by Williams. "Account of Presbyterian Mission," 136.

active & brisk, was filled with Pity for ym in their present State of Heathenism, was surprized to see ym after they were all in a Leather with sweat, having Danced an Hour together run out into ye cold Air to cool ymselves & sometimes into the River, wc occasions great Colds among ym.

Richardson later was welcomed to Keowee at the Town House. The visitor shook hands and "measured arms" with his hosts. After "smoking out of the beloved Pipe" and being shown "Belts of wampum wc preserve the Talk of different Nations to them [the Cherokees], & their Signs of Friendship," the traveler spoke of Christianity. He did not record the reaction of the natives to his sermon, but he was asked to intercede with the "Governor" [evidently of South Carolina] in order to renew peace between the Cherokees and the Catawbas. The Cherokees had recently executed a Catawba but did not desire warfare.[17]

Richardson did not mention the construction of private homes or the physical arrangement of Cherokee villages, but he did comment on some of the social mores and religious customs. He noted that Chota was a "Beloved Town" where no violence was permitted. According to him, the rule applied to all circumstances; even prisoners of war were taken outside Chota for execution. Native religious beliefs were of decided interest to the missionary, and he was especially curious to learn of the Cherokee "sacred fire." In mid-January, 1759, he observed a dance which he believed to be "some religious Ceremony paid to the Fire, as they frequently bowed to it." He was told, however, that the gestures were "only a Custom they have & they don't seem to worship anything." Whether his informant was an English trader or an Indian is not apparent, but he later learned that the ceremonial fire was called "grand Father, because of its warmth in winter." The minister did not reveal the source of that information, but it was evidently a Cherokee man. On another occasion, Richardson had a long discussion with an Indian concerning Christianity and native religion. One of them admitted that some Cherokees "talked" to the fire, " & it to their Father above, others to ye Water." The man con-

[17] Richardson, "Diary," Dec. 18, 29, 1758; Feb. 16, 1759.

tinued with a hint of a Cherokee legend. The white recorded that "he said the Moon stole all her light from the Sun & all was water at first." The traveler observed the preparation of a "Physick" but gave few details. He mentioned that the Indians sought the blessing of the "great Man above" and fasted before using the concoction. He did not record who prepared the drink, its ingredients, or its purpose.[18]

The Presbyterian missionary earnestly sought to interest the Cherokees in Christianity. He realized that they had a definite standard of moral behavior, which the minister termed their "good Thot [thought]." He endeavored to use the native concept of morality to show the need for accepting the white man's religion, but he received little encouragement. The Indians were fascinated by some illustrations of Biblical themes and expressed the hope that Richardson's religion could be used to defeat enemies or rival ball players; however, most were simply indifferent. A few were openly hostile to his efforts. One young warrior criticized the supposedly Christian traders and told Richardson's interpreter "what does he [Richardson] talk to me for, the Town does not desire to hear yt Talk, let him stay till he talks publicly & yn we shall all hear." Greatly discouraged, the minister concluded the entry with: "so now they seem adverse to hear by ymselves, the only way I had to communicate Instructions to them, what can I do, O Lord, do thou direct me."[19]

William Richardson left the Cherokee nation thoroughly discouraged with the prospects of working for their salvation. Probably by chance, the missionary had come into close contact with three leaders of the anti-English faction within the nation—Oconostota, or the Great Warrior, and Standing Turkey of the Overhill settlements, and Wawhatchee, First Warrior of the Lower Cherokees. Unlike the Reverend Mr. John Martin, Richardson was never permitted to preach openly. The second Presbyterian missionary had avoided

[18] *Ibid.*, Jan. 11, 14, 17, 18, 23, 27, 1759. On the Cherokee Fire Ceremony, see David H. Corkran, "The Sacred Fires of the Cherokees," *Southern Indian Studies*, Vol. V (Oct., 1953), 21–26.

[19] *Ibid.*, Jan. 14, 17, 22, 24, 27, 30; Feb. 20, 1759.

trouble with the influential shamans with whom Martin had quarreled, but conditions within the nation had changed rapidly during the winter of 1758–59. Richardson departed correctly believing that war was coming between the Cherokees and the English. The Indians knew of the murder of some of their tribesmen by white Virginians, and although he did not stress the fact, the minister realized that the natives had learned of his coming from the Old Dominion. Little Carpenter, one of England's most devoted friends in the nation, had been disgraced, and Richardson entertained little hope that the Cherokee Second Man could continue to restrain the war fever.[20]

Richardson placed much of the blame on the English for the possibility of war. He criticized the traders for generally setting a bad example. He was once forced to lock his door against Indians drunk on English rum. Moreover, twice during his short sojourn among the Indians, a trader killed a native.[21] But despite such offenses, the traveler believed that white intrusion into the Indians' land and food supply was more important as a cause of native hostility. He denounced the frontiersmen who settled "30 or 40 miles" inside Indian territory or killed the game so that the red men were "naked." Richardson optimistically believed that the encroachments could be prevented. According to him, "how easy it is for the government to restrain these idle fellows & it won't hurt the public & take away their [the Cherokees'] cause of complaint before it be too late."[22]

At the end of the diary, which was sent to the Presbyterian Indian Society, the missionary listed three reasons for his resignation from the Cherokee mission. First, he was not willing to arm himself,

[20] *Ibid.*, Jan. 5, 14; Feb. 1, 3, 20, 27, 1759; concluding entry, undated but probably Mar. 17, 1759; Corkran, *Cherokee Frontier*, 194, 218–21 *et passim*; and Alden, *John Stuart*, 104–105, 116–18.

[21] Richardson, "Diary," Jan. 11, 22; Feb. 5, 24, 1759. The Reverend Mr. Charles Woodmason believed that Richardson was forced to leave his mission because of the opposition of the traders. Charles Woodmason, *Carolina Backcountry on the Eve of the Revolution*, ed. Richard J. Hooker, 133. However, there is very little if any support for the belief in the diary. Instead of opposing him, the traders shared their homes and food and acted as interpreters for the missionary. "Diary," Dec. 7, 10, 14, 29, 1758.

[22] *Ibid.*, Jan. 30, 1759.

which he believed was necessary for protection in a missionary's travels. Second, his "Constitution" was not robust, and a minister to the Indians was often forced to travel and live under adverse conditions. Third, by his resigning, "a better Person" could continue the effort. Richardson was probably too hard on himself. He was often ill during his travels, and occasionally he did fear bodily harm, but when he closed the journal he was considering going to the Catawba Indians as a missionary. The degree of uncertainty in undertaking another Indian mission was apparent in the writing, and almost certainly he did not conduct extensive work among the Catawbas. Richardson soon had a church at Waxhaw, South Carolina, and before his death, which occurred about 1777, he founded several Presbyterian churches in western South Carolina.[23]

The recorded impressions of the Southern Indians by young George Washington, Andrew Burnaby, and William Richardson were quite diverse. The encounters and observations of Washington and Burnaby were extremely limited. They recorded only the most obvious aspects of Indian life and gave little indication of their reactions. Richardson gained a far greater knowledge of the Indians, but his interests centered on one aspect of native civilization: religion. He went to the Cherokee nation sincerely desirous of preaching Christianity to the natives but was greatly disappointed at the lack of interest. The missionary attributed the failure of his activities to the increasing antagonism between the English and the Cherokees; however, he realized only dimly, if at all, a more basic obstacle to his efforts. Christianity was, of course, a vital element in European culture and society, and the Indians' religion was equally essential in native civilization. Both the Catawbas, who were at peace with the English, and the Cherokees, who were approaching open warfare, had little concern for the white man's God and his means of salvation.

The war foreseen by Richardson came within a year of his

[23] *Ibid.*, Mar. 14, 1759; concluding entry; Williams, "Account of Presbyterian Mission," 129; and Brown, *Catawba Indians*, 246.

return to the white settlements. When peace was restored in the autumn of 1761, Henry Timberlake, a young Virginia militiaman, volunteered to visit the Cherokees as a visible sign of the renewed friendship. From his observations he wrote one of the best colonial accounts of the Southeastern Indians.

X

Henry Timberlake and the Cherokees

IN January, 1760, the war that William Richardson had feared began. There were attacks upon the English traders among the Lower and Middle Cherokees, and Fort Prince George was besieged. In February the Overhill Cherokees joined the fighting, although some, including Little Carpenter, refused to take part in the hostilities. The events of early 1760 actually constituted a declaration of open warfare on the part of the Indians and followed a year of sporadic raiding by small war parties. After two years of warfare during which the Cherokees raided through the Southern frontier and two expeditions of British redcoats and Carolina militia destroyed Lower and Middle Cherokee villages and fields, peace was restored in late 1761.[1]

During the fighting, a force of Virginia militia under Colonel William Byrd III had moved slowly westward toward the Overhill Cherokees. On August 1, 1761, Byrd resigned his command. Under his successor, Lieutenant Colonel Adam Stephen, the force advanced to Great Island on the Holston River and constructed Fort Robinson. In the autumn of 1761, Standing Turkey, who had become the Fire

[1] An interesting contemporary account of the beginning and first year of the war is William Fyffe, "Letter to Brother John, February 1, 1761," Manuscript Collection of Thomas Gilcrease Institute of American History and Art, Tulsa, Oklahoma. The institute has kindly made a photostat of the letter available to the writer. The definitive study of the loss of Cherokee friendship and the war is Corkran, *Cherokee Frontier*.

King of the Cherokees after the death of Old Hop in 1759, and a few companions traveled to the island seeking to negotiate peace with the English. Colonel Stephen informed the Cherokees that peace could only be made with the Carolinians, but he entertained the Indians for several weeks. In November news that the fighting had ceased reached Great Island, and the Cherokees, who had enjoyed the Virginians' hospitality, reluctantly prepared to return home. Standing Turkey requested that as a gesture of good faith an Englishman travel to the Overhills' villages. The plan was approved, and a volunteer was sought. Ensign Henry Timberlake of the Virginia militia agreed to make the long and possibly hazardous journey.

Henry Timberlake was born in 1730 in Hanover County, Virginia, and in 1756 he joined the Virginia militia regiment commanded by Colonel George Washington. Two years later he served during the Forbes campaign against Fort Duquesne in Colonel Byrd's regiment and remained in the regiment during the expedition against the Cherokees. In the spring of 1762 Timberlake returned to Virginia with a large party of Indians. In May, the ensign, two other whites, and three Cherokees sailed for London. The voyage across the Atlantic was apparently undertaken at the request of one of the Cherokees, Ostenaco, who desired fame similar to that gained by the Indian members of Sir Alexander Cuming's party in 1730. Timberlake evidently financed the trip himself, and in Great Britain he was criticized for charging the curious to see the native Americans. The attempt to profit from the Cherokees was unsuccessful, and because of the lack of money, the ensign remained in England when the Indians returned home. Timberlake married in England and traveled to America to rejoin his regiment, but he was soon retired as a lieutenant at half pay. When the Virginia Council refused to reimburse him for his expenses in the Cherokee country, he once more sailed for London. There he wrote an account of the Cherokees, but his death on September 30, 1765, may have occurred before his work was published.[2]

[2] Henry Timberlake, *Lieut. Henry Timberlake's Memoirs*, ed. Samuel C. Williams, 130–33, 155–68.

Timberlake began his *Memoirs* with a map of the Overhill Cherokee country and included a list of village chiefs and the number of warriors, which was slightly more than eight hundred at the time of his visit. In the remainder of the work, he described his journeys to and from the Cherokee nation and his impressions of native civilization gained during his three-month residence among the Indians.

After leaving Fort Robinson on November 28, 1761, Timberlake, three other Englishmen, and a small band of Cherokees traveled by water to Chota, the most important Overhill town. The water passage was undertaken despite the objections of Standing Turkey, who wanted the whites to accompany him overland, because Timberlake wanted to learn an all water route to the Cherokee nation. At the end of twenty-two days of traveling down the Holston River and then up the Little Tennessee River, the ensign achieved his goal, but the journey was extremely difficult. The weather was very cold, and because the rivers were low, the men frequently had to pull the canoe through the frigid water and over sand bars. At one point, it alternately snowed, hailed, and rained on the party, and after one gun was lost and the only other one was broken, the travelers nearly ran out of food. But the remaining gun was repaired, and the guide managed to kill a bear. On December 14 the whites encountered a Cherokee hunting party and finished the journey under its direction.[3]

During his first few days among the Cherokees, Timberlake was enthusiastically welcomed, despite the recent hostilities between the Indians and the English. For example, Ostenaco, to whom the writer referred by his title of "Outacity," gave him "a general invitation to his house." The Indian probably hoped to increase his influence with the English, but the visitor appreciated the hospitality. At Settico, a town on the Little Tennessee River near Chota, the ensign was greeted by several hundred painted Indians who danced and sang as expressions of their joy. He was also welcomed with gifts of beads and speeches at Settico. In his description of the welcome, Timberlake

---

[3] *Ibid.*, 40–57. The Cherokees who began the trip with the Englishmen seem to have left them at some point in the journey.

Cherokees Who Accompanied Sir Alexander Cuming to London in 1730. Engraving by Isaac Basire after painting by Markham.

Courtesy of the Smithsonian Institution National Anthropological Archives, Bureau of American Ethnology Collection

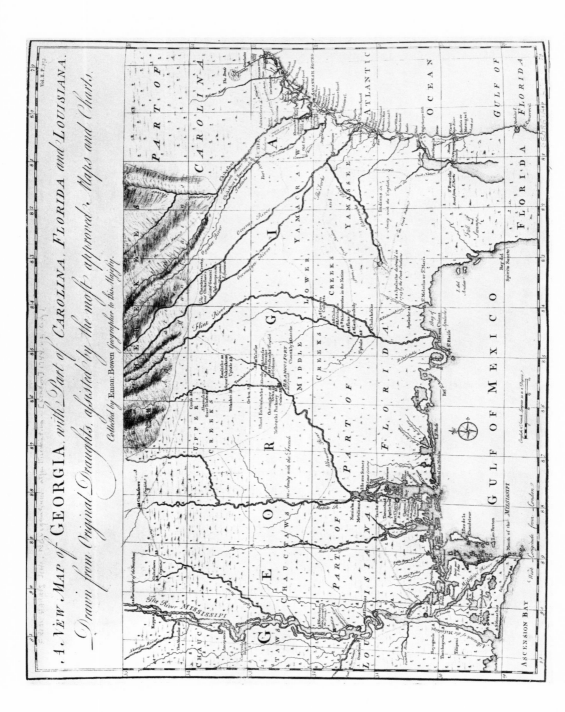

Emanuel Bowen, *A New Map of Georgia*, 1748. The attempt of the cartographer to show the attitude of the various Indian tribes toward the English is unusual for the period.

Courtesy of the Rare Book Division, The New York Public Library, Astor, Lenox, and Tilden Foundations.

Bernard Romans, *Creek and Choctaw Pictographs.* Romans indicated that the drawing on the left was made by a Creek war party, but offered no explanation of the Choctaw drawing on the right. Pictographs were more common in the Southeast than the comments by colonial travelers would indicate.

Courtesy of the Smithsonian Institution National Anthropological Archives, Bureau of American Ethnology Collection

Bernard Romans, *Head of Chickasaw Warrior*.
Courtesy of the Smithsonian Institution National Anthropological Archives, Bureau of
American Ethnology Collection

Bernard Romans, *Two Busts of Choctaw Indians.*
Courtesy of the Smithsonian Institution National Anthropological Archives, Bureau of American Ethnology Collection

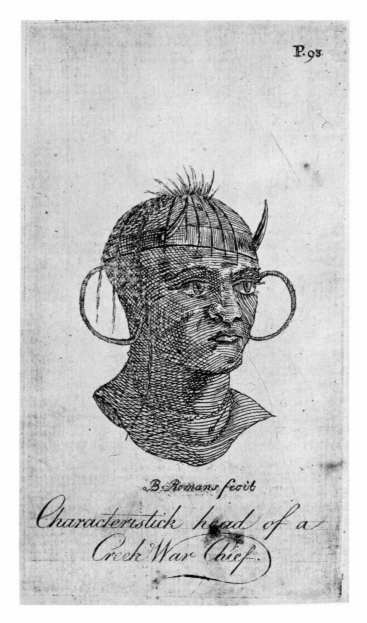

Bernard Romans, *Head of a Creek War Chief*.
Courtesy of the Smithsonian Institution National Anthropological
Archives, Bureau of American Ethnology Collection

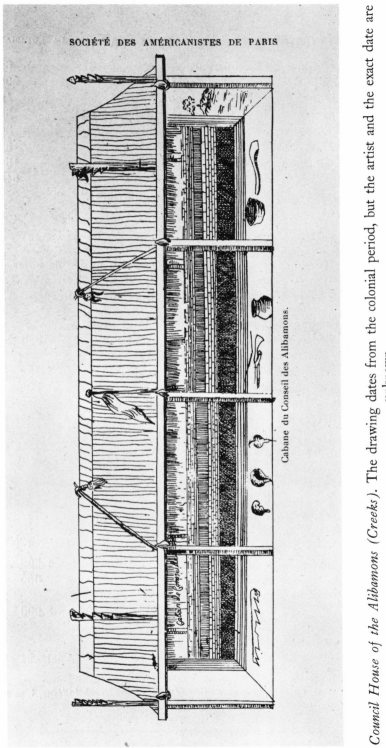

SOCIÉTÉ DES AMÉRICANISTES DE PARIS

Cabane du Conseil des Alibamons.

Council House of the Alibamons (Creeks). The drawing dates from the colonial period, but the artist and the exact date are unknown.

Courtesy of the Smithsonian Institution National Anthropological Archives, Bureau of American Ethnology Collection

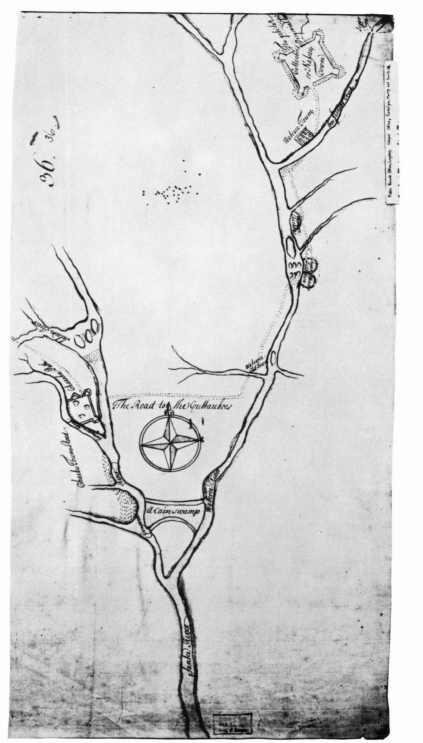

Santee River Area Showing the Catawba Villages, ca. 1750. The cartographer is unknown. William Richardson traveled through the area a few years after the map was drawn.

Courtesy of the Library of Congress

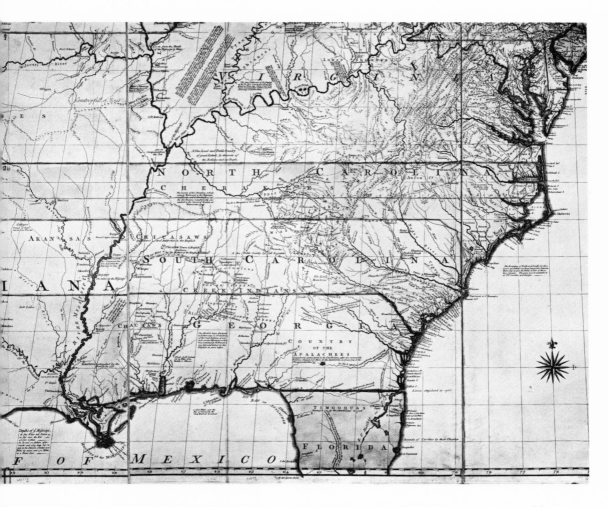

John Mitchell, *A Map of the British and French Dominions in North America,* 1755. The Mitchell map, of which only a portion is shown, was one of the most important maps of the eighteenth century.

Courtesy of the Library of Congress

An Account of my Proceedings
since I accepted the Indian Mission
in October 2d. 1758. to go & exercise my office as a Minister among
the Cherokees or any other Indian
Nation that would allow me to preach
to them.
Oct 2d. 1758
New-Castle, Hanover. Virginia

I set out from Newcastle to wait upon the Governor, & Council to sollicite
their recommendation to ye Comman-
dants of the Forts in the Cherokee
Nation, & to get their approbation of
ye Instructions given me by the Society here after such corrections & amend-
ments as they should think proper.
got into Wmsburgh in the Evening.
in company with the Revd. Mr Davies
& Mr George Webb a member of the Society for managing the mission & Schools
among ye Indians. rode about 50 mils
rained very hard upon us some of the
Way.
Wm. burgh Tuesday Octr 3. Intended to
have waited upon the Governor this
Morning, but had rode out on acct
of his Health, & was not to return
till one of ye Clock. It was judged
proper to wait upon him this

Page from William Richardson, *An Account of My Proceedings*,
1758.
Courtesy of the Manuscript Division, The New York Public Library, Astor,
Lenox, and Tilden Foundations

THE
MEMOIRS
OF
Lieut. HENRY TIMBERLAKE,

(Who accompanied the Three Cherokee Indians to England in the Year 1762)

CONTAINING

Whatever he obſerved remarkable, or worthy of public Notice, during his Travels to and from that Nation; wherein the Country, Government, Genius, and Cuſtoms of the Inhabitants, are authentically deſcribed.

ALSO

The PRINCIPAL OCCURRENCES during their Reſidence in LONDON.

Illuſtrated with

An ACCURATE MAP of their Over-hill Settlement, and a curious Secret JOURNAL, taken by the Indians out of the Pocket of a Frenchman they had killed.

LONDON:

Printed for the AUTHOR; and ſold by J. RIDLEY, in St. James's-Street; W. NICOLL, in St. Paul's Church-Yard; and C. HENDERSON, at the Royal-Exchange.
MDCCLXV.

Title Page of Henry Timberlake, *The Memoirs of Lieut. Henry Timberlake*, 1765.
Courtesy of the Library of Congress

Tellassee

Part of Tellassee

Chilhowey

Half way Town

Enemy Mountains

Settacoo

Four Mile Creek

Path from Virginia

CHOTE *the Metropolis*

To Charles Town

A Fort
Built by the Virginians 1756
and soon after destroyed by the Indians.

Tennessee

Tennessee River

Toqua

Ball play Creek

Tommotley

Toskegee

Fort Loudon

Tellequo River

A Draught of the
CHEROKEE COUNTRY,

On the West Side of the Twenty four Mountains,
commonly called Over the Hills;
Taken by Henry Timberlake, when he
was in that Country, in March 1762.

Likewise the

Names of the Principal or Head men of each Town, and
what Number of Fighting Men they send to War.

Mialaquo. or the } 24 under the Governor of Attakullakulla.
Great Island....}

Toskegee........ 55 Attakullakulla Governor.

Tommotley...... 91 Ostenaco Commander in Chief.

Toqua .... 82 Willinawaw Governor.

Tennessee....... 21 under the Goverment of Kanagatuckco.

Chote .... 175 Kanagatuckco King & Governor.

Chilhowey...... 110 Yachtino Governor.

Settacoo....... 204 Cheulah Governor

Tellassee...... 47 Governor dead & none elected since.
         ‾‾‾
         809

Mialaquo or
Great Island

A Scale of Miles.

1   2   3

Henry Timberlake, *A Draught of the Cherokee Country,* 1765.
Courtesy of the Library of Congress

The Three Cherokees came over from the head of the River Savanna to London 1762.
I. their Interpreter that was Poisoned.

The Three Cherokees Came Over from the Head of the River Savanna, 1762. These Indians, who accompanied Timberlake to London, were identified as Outacite or Man-Killer (left), Austenaco or King (center), and Uschesees the Great Hunter or Scalper. To the extreme left is the interpreter who was "poisoned." Engraving from an unknown source.

Courtesy of the Smithsonian Institution National Anthropological Archives, Bureau of American Ethnology Collection

Outacite, Chief of the Cherokees, 1762. Engraving from an unknown
source.
Courtesy of the Smithsonian Institution National Anthropological Archives, Bureau
of American Ethnology Collection

Austenaco, Great Warrior, 1762. Engraving from *Royal Magazine* from portrait by Sir Joshua Reynolds.

Cunne Shote, 1762. Painting by F. Parsons.
Courtesy of the Smithsonian Institution National Anthropological Archives, Bureau of American Ethnology Collection

noted that a few men in the large gathering were nearly naked and all of them were "painted all over in a hideous manner." The headsman was especially striking. His entire body was painted "blood-red" except for his face, half of which was painted black. In the Settico Town House the visitor was entertained by four male dancers whose bodies were "painted milk white." In the *Memoirs*, the author also gave a good picture of the ordinary appearance of the natives. Of the men he wrote:

> The Cherokees are of a middle stature of an olive colour, tho' generally painted, and their skins stained with gunpowder, pricked into it in many pretty figures. The hair of their head is shaved, tho' many of the old people have it plucked out by the roots, except a patch on the hinder part of the head, about twice the bigness of a crown-piece, which is ornamented with beads, feathers, wampum.

The Englishman continued by indicating that the ear lobes were "split" and stretched. Ornaments were attached to the enlarged lobes. Other jewelry included necklaces and bracelets of silver and shell. Women as well as men were fond of the ornaments. Women permitted their hair to grow long and often decorated it with ribbons. Finally, Timberlake praised the beauty of the women, especially those with some European blood.[4]

The Virginia militia officer was naturally interested in Indian warfare. He noted a variety of weapons being used by the Indians and indicated that "tommahawkes" were found in several shapes and were entirely of European origin by the mid-eighteenth century. He believed that women occasionally fought alongside the men. In Timberlake's opinion, the cruel punishment inflicted by the women on prisoners returned to the villages was worse than the fighting. Indirectly, Timberlake probably revealed a decline in native population when he stated that in recent years it had become common for prisoners to be married into the tribe rather than executed. War and peace were decided upon by councils, and if the decision was to fight, a blood-stained tomahawk was raised; if peace was to come, the weapon was

4 *Ibid.*, 58, 63–64, 75–77.

buried. In the councils, a man's oratorical ability was of highest importance, and the traveler praised the speaking ability of the Cherokees. After war was declared, an ornate club or hatchet was taken into the enemy's territory and left where it would be found. The gesture was a challenge to the enemy to return the weapon to the Cherokees. Timberlake witnessed the return of a successful war party against the Shawnees and described the event. Upon entering the village the braves danced around the Town House three times while singing a war chant and shouting the "Death Hallow." Meanwhile, four scalps painted red were held aloft. The writer reported that, unlike European officers, the leader of a native expedition brought up the rear during marches. In the Town House the party's exploits were exuberantly narrated and the war dances completed. Perhaps as an afterthought, the traveler included a translation of one war song in a footnote in his *Memoirs*.[5]

During his sojourn the ensign witnessed several ceremonies and many dances, and he especially favored the war dances and the "pantomime dances." One such "pantomime" was the enactment of a bear hunt. Two men wore bear skins and two others acted as hunters, and together they enacted the killing of the large beasts. He also saw an Eagle Dance but gave no real description, although it was the Cherokees' most important dance. He did, however, realize the great value placed on eagle feathers, which were used ceremonially in treaty negotiations and in several rituals. The white visitor indicated that great honor awaited the warrior who obtained such feathers. Such men were awarded the title of "Colona," the second highest title in the nation, and were given many gifts.

Timberlake observed what he called the "green corn dance," which was held in the town square. The graceful motions of the people and their song "to God for the corn he has sent them" pleased the visitor, although he reported few details of the dance. He did give a more vivid picture of a "physic-dance," essentially a cleansing ritual. It centered around a concoction of herbs and roots prepared by a Be-

[5] *Ibid.*, 59–60, 77–82, 113.

loved Woman. A conjurer or shaman had purified the undertaking before the preparation, and further ceremony attended its drinking. After about an hour's dancing, the people began to drink and Timberlake was invited to participate. To his surprise, he was pleased at the sassafras taste of the mixture.

Timberlake also believed that a ceremonial form of charity had religious meaning. He related that a poverty-stricken family would provide music for a dance. After each warrior had related a courageous feat, the music would stop, and the man would place an item of some value, "a string of wampum, piece of plate, wire, paint, lead, or any thing he can most conveniently spare," on a skin. Next, the process would be repeated. Although Timberlake stated that the ritual was a part of the Cherokee religion, he did not include the reason for his opinion.[6]

The sharing of tobacco was an important part of many rituals, and the Virginian smoked many pipes. Describing one pipe, he wrote:

the bowl of it was red stone, curiously cut with a knife, it being very soft, tho' extremely pretty when polished. Some of these [pipes] are of black stone, and some earth they make their pots with, but beautifully diversified. The stem is about three feet long.

Timberlake also mentioned that tomahawks frequently had an opening through the handle and back so that they could be used as pipes. He did not indicate whether such dual-purpose weapons were largely ceremonial, but they were mentioned in connection with warfare.[7]

The Virginian disliked the shamans, who were vital to much of the native ceremonial life. He blamed them for causing the departure of John Martin, the Presbyterian missionary. Once, a conjurer proclaimed that he had "found" a missing bolt of broadcloth, but the

---

[6] *Ibid.*, 88–89, 92–93, 100–103, 107. On Cherokee religious and ceremonial life, see Gilbert, "Eastern Cherokees," 261–63, 325–44 *et passim*; Mooney, "Myths of the Cherokees," 229–427; and James Mooney, "The Sacred Formulas of the Cherokees," BAE *Seventh Annual Report*, 318–97.

[7] Timberlake, *Memoirs*, 65, 77–78.

white traveler believed that the man had taken the material in order to pretend to find it. Elsewhere, he described the use of "conjuring stones" in certain rites. One stone had special meaning, because it was supposedly from the "head of a monstrous serpent." The shaman who possessed it told of a courageous warrior who slayed the serpent to obtain the "jewel." Timberlake never saw the stone, but he did believe it existed. He was, however, highly skeptical of the tale and disliked the conjurer's use of it to give the stone great value. From his comments, it was apparent that Timberlake realized the "stones" had special meaning to the Cherokees. The belief in a Great Horned Serpent and the supernatural qualities of "stones" obtained from such beings was very much a part of Cherokee mythology, but he displayed little appreciation for the natives' religion.[8]

Ignorance of the mythological significance of the "sacred stone" was understandable on the part of a visitor, but Timberlake's errors concerning Cherokee burial practices were more surprising. According to him, the Overhills greatly feared the dead and often hired Europeans to dispose of corpses. The whites received a blanket and such items as they could take from the burial offering. The writer also believed that Indians occasionally took offerings from graves, although such desecrations were considered "the worst of thefts." He indicated that the usual place of burial was in rivers. Yet, the Cherokees seldom if ever buried the dead in rivers, and although they considered a corpse to be "unclean," they evidently did not have any unusual fear of the dead.[9]

Despite the existence of influential shamans and traditional ceremonies, Henry Timberlake believed that Cherokee religion contained a large amount of individualism within a generally held concept of "one superior being." In a passage that summarized his opinion, he wrote:

As to religion, every one is at liberty to think for himself; whence flows a diversity of opinions amongst those that do think, but the major part

[8] *Ibid.*, 74, 87–88, 127; and Mooney, "Myths of the Cherokees," 458–61.
[9] Timberlake, *Memoirs*, 90–91; and Gilbert, "Eastern Cherokee," 347–48.

do not give themselves that trouble. They generally concur, however, in the belief of one superior Being, who made them, and governs all things, and are therefore never discontent at any misfortune, because they say, the Man above would have it so.[10]

The writer also discussed other elements within Cherokee society and culture. He did not entertain a high opinion of Indians as craftsmen, but from his remarks it was apparent that he was referring primarily to the production of items of European origin. He did praise several native skills. The Virginian discussed the dugout canoes used on the rivers. Some of the canoes, thirty or forty feet long, were capable of carrying fifteen or twenty men, yet they were light in weight and easy to manage. The pre-European method of fashioning a boat from a pine or poplar tree trunk had been to remove slowly and carefully the wood with fire and stone implements. But the natives had adopted iron tools by the time of Timberlake's sojourn. The author also discussed at some length the making of bows and arrows. Arrows were of reeds, and the heads were made of "thin brass, copper, bone, or scales of a particular fish." Bows were made of various types of wood and were seasoned by heat and the application of bear's oil. A "twisted bear's gut" was used as the string. Timberlake observed a pottery of "red" and "white" clays but made no comment upon the method of construction or the shapes of the vessels. Some of the women had also learned to make cloth and could sew European-style clothing.

Timberlake was also impressed by the Town Houses and homes of the Overhill Cherokees. The Town House was made of wooden poles covered with earth and shaped like a "sugar loaf." It was quite large, and the visitor estimated that five hundred persons could find places within the building. Because of its construction and size, Timberlake said, the Town House looked like "a small mountain at a little distance." Having no windows or chimney, the smoke escaping from a hole in the roof, Town Houses were dark and smoky. He noted also that two large flags were flown from the structures; white flags were used in time of peace, red whenever the nation was at

[10] Timberlake, *Memoirs*, 87.

war. The private houses were made of upright poles with smaller sticks interwoven "like a basket" and covered with clay. The resulting walls were "very smooth and sometimes white-washed." The houses were also warm, dark, and smoky. Many were quite large, being sixty to seventy feet in length and about one-fifth as high. Within the dwelling, furniture was sparse, and beds were merely boards covered with bear skins. Little if any covering was needed while sleeping because of the heat. A sweat or hot house was usually attached to the home. Whereas the houses were merely quite warm, the sweat houses were extremely hot because of a constant fire.[11]

Timberlake was evidently well fed during his visit, and he highly praised the food of the natives. At one point in the *Memoirs* he described a meal. He had a choice of venison, bear, or buffalo meat, potatoes, pumpkins, corn, peas, and beans. There was no silverware, but small flat baskets of split cane were used as dishes. Elsewhere, the visitor commented on Cherokee bread making. According to him,

after making a fire on the hearth-stone, about the size of a large dish, they sweep the embers off, laying a loaf smooth on it; this they cover with a sort of deep dish, and renew the fire upon the whole, under which the bread bakes to as great perfection as in any European oven.

He realized that some of the food was not of American origin but was mistaken on one item. He believed that

before the arrival of the Europeans, the natives were not so well provided, maize, melons, and tobacco, being the only things they bestowed culture upon, and perhaps seldom on the latter.

In the same passage Timberlake named melons as well as "pumpkins" and was obviously not confusing the two. His remark may indicate the rapid acceptance of melons by the natives. Had the ensign substituted "pumpkins" for "melons" he would have indicated three of the most important aboriginal plants cultivated in the Southeast. He also noted the abundance of cherry, peach, pear, and plum orchards. He greatly praised the richness of the soil tilled by the Cherokees and

[11] *Ibid.*, 59–64, 83–85.

evidently believed that the fertility explained the division of labor among the Indians. He remarked that the "women do all the laborious tasks of agriculture, the soil requiring only a little stirring with a hoe, to produce whatever is required of it." In reality, women did most of the horticulture, but men helped with the planting and harvesting and perhaps with some of the cultivation. If the traveler was aware that the horticultural methods of the Indians exhausted the soil at least as quickly as the crude farming of the white colonials, he did not comment upon the fact.[12]

In addition to horticulture, the Cherokees depended heavily upon hunting and fishing for their subsistence. The Virginian noted that the natives fished with lines and spears and obtained large numbers of fish by constructing two dams across the smaller streams. When the barriers were finished, the people entered the water upstream and drove the fish into the reservoir. The opening was blocked "with a large brush, or bundle made on purpose," and the fish were taken in baskets. Hunting was more important to the Cherokees than fishing. Although Timberlake mentioned several animals used as food, he did not discuss hunting techniques. Probably because it was something of a novelty, he did note that young boys often hunted with blowguns. The weapons were made of "sarbacan, or hollow cane." They were not powerful, but the youths were proficient in hitting the eyes of animals and thereby capturing their quarry. With such early training, Timberlake felt, the men had an easy life; their only responsibilities were "hunting, and warring abroad, and lazying at home."[13]

The government of the Overhills was another element of native society described by Timberlake. His concept of Cherokee political organization was summarized when he said that "their government, if I may call it government, which has neither laws or power to support it, is a mixed aristocracy and democracy." He continued by explaining that each warrior could express his opinion and that a few, the "aristocracy," had the most persuasive power. The leaders were not heredi-

---

[12] *Ibid.*, 57, 61, 68–70; and Swanton, *Southeastern Indians*, I, 284–86.
[13] Timberlake, *Memoirs*, 69, 71–72, 99.

tary; instead, they gained fame and influence because they were best at fighting or wisest in councils. Interestingly, Timberlake indicated that women occasionally took part in war expeditions and thereby gained unusual respect. Within the aristocracy there were grades. Those men who were considered to have the greatest ability as warriors were given the title of "Outacity, or Man-killer, and the second, Colona, or the Raven." The traveler also noted that the capture of an eagle earned a man the rank of "Colona." Women could not earn either of these titles, but they could be granted the title of "Beloved," which was also given men past the age of fighting. The Virginian observed two factions among the Overhills and noted that the groups usually were in disagreement. He probably had reference to the important Red and White organizations that existed in Cherokee society, but his meaning is not entirely clear. Furthermore, he believed that the Indians had little love for the English and considered the French more successful in gaining Cherokee friendship. The Cherokees realized the need for English trade goods, however, and were adept at playing one European power against the other in order to gain greater advantage.[14]

A few other aspects of native civilization were more briefly mentioned by Henry Timberlake. He believed that Cherokee marriages usually had little permanence and that "it is common for a person to change [spouses] three or four times a year." Some marriages did last for lifetimes, and he praised the loyalty of the Indian wives of the Fort Loudoun soldiers who had furnished food during the siege of the fort in the recent war with the English. The ensign correctly realized that all children were retained by the mother, but he evidently was ignorant of the true importance of women in the matri-centered society of the Cherokees. Mothers were praised for the care given to infants. The writer lacked an understanding of Cherokee social organization, with its matrilineal clans, but he did note that the punishment for murder was left to the family of the deceased.

One form of Cherokee recreation was indicated in the *Memoirs*. Timberlake observed a game of "nettecawaw," a version of

[14] *Ibid.*, 93–98, 103; and Gilbert, "Eastern Cherokees," 317–56.

the widely-distributed Southeastern game of chunkey. A smooth stone disc was rolled along the ground, and two players threw long poles after it. The object was to hit the stone or land near where it stopped and to prevent the opponent from doing so. The game was not all in fun; heavy gambling attended the playing of it.[15]

Timberlake's general impression of the Indians was not apparent. He praised the hospitality of the Cherokees but considered them gluttons in eating and drinking. They loved to gamble, and many had become addicted to the Europeans' liquor, but they were "hardy" and often lived to be very old. The visitor believed that his hosts were not interested in religious speculation or any theoretical thought, but they quickly accepted useful European introductions such as horses, cattle, swine, and certain vegetables and fruits. They were a proud people who preferred to deal with "officers" and not the "lower class of Europeans"; yet native wives were loyal to their soldier husbands in time of war between the two races.

The statement that the Overhill Cherokees were not speculative might also be applied to Timberlake. The *Memoirs* were almost entirely descriptive. Timberlake made little attempt to evaluate or understand the civilization of his hosts. Unlike other Englishmen who wrote at length on the Indian, he did not enter the controversy about the origin of the native Americans. He noted that a native acquired little if any property by inheritance and indicated his belief that it was common throughout North America and parts of Asia to leave nothing to heirs. If he was indirectly revealing his support for an Asian origin of the Indians, he did not develop the thought.[16]

Henry Timberlake recorded many elements in the life of the Cherokees. Appearance of the natives, their warfare, government, and religion received the most attention. The soil and natural products of the Cherokee country were highly praised, and an Englishman reading the newly-published work in 1765 would have gained a most favorable impression of a part of the area so recently acknowledged by

[15] Timberlake, *Memoirs*, 89–90, 99–100.
[16] *Ibid.*, 31, 68, 72, 78–80, 87.

Spain and France as solely the possession of Great Britain. The author of the *Memoirs* failed to benefit in any monetary way from the book, but he left to posterity one of the best accounts of the Southeastern Indians to be written during the colonial period of American history.

XI

Conclusion

THE British travelers who visited the Southern Indians between 1660 and 1763 exhibited both diverse and common attributes. They shared a willingness to undertake tiresome and frequently hazardous journeys, and with few exceptions they did not undertake the trips for pleasure. Only about one-third of the men made trips specifically to visit Indian groups. These travelers included government officials such as Indian Commissioners George Chicken and John Herbert, ministers such as Francis Le Jau and William Richardson, and the "official" visitor, Henry Timberlake. In the period immediately following 1660 several men such as John Lederer and Henry Woodward journeyed into the wilderness to gain knowledge of the land and the possibilities of trade with the Indians. Less than half of the men made journeys having nothing to do with the native Americans, encountering them only incidentally in the course of the trip. These included several early colonists of South Carolina and Georgia, four men seeking converts to the Society of Friends, the young George Washington, and the well-to-do Andrew Burnaby.

The Virginia gentleman Robert Beverley, who visited the Indians solely out of curiosity, was unusual. John Lawson and the Scottish baronet Sir Alexander Cuming contended that they traveled among the Indians for pleasure, but evidence seems to indicate the presence of other reasons. Lawson was interested in the possibilities of trade. Cuming may not have had clearly defined motives for his journey, but he probably hoped to profit materially from the experience. The reason for some of the travels are not known. This is true of the accounts written by the indentured servant George Alsop, the surgeon Thomas Glover, "R.F.," and the anonymous account by the early eighteenth-century traveler in Maryland.

A common characteristic of these visits was their length. None of the sojourns lasted for more than a few months, except for Gabriel Arthur's. Arthur remained among the "Tomahitans" for slightly more than a year, and although he was not an actual captive, it appears that he was not entirely at liberty to return to the English settlements whenever he desired. Aside from Arthur's, the longest visit appears to have been that of the Creek agent Tobias Fitch, who remained for five months. The majority of the encounters lasted less than a month, and several lasted only a few days.

Most of the travelers seem to have been educated men. Approximately one-third of them were college graduates, and most of the others appear to have been better educated than most of their contemporaries. Most of the British colonists who encountered the Southern Indians did not record their impressions, but, as might be expected, those who did make the effort were generally erudite.

The professions of the white travelers were diverse. One-fourth of them were ministers in the Church of England and the Presbyterian Church and leaders of the Society of Friends. Nearly as many of the visitors held government positions. These individuals included a governor of South Carolina, two minor officials of the Georgia colony, and three men holding posts specifically concerned with Indian affairs. Other accounts were written by two sea captains, two surgeons, two Virginia plantation owners, a surveyor, and a militia officer. An English gentleman and a Scottish nobleman also left their impressions of the Indians. Only one of the writers, the unknown "Ranger" who recorded the expedition of James Oglethorpe to the Creeks in 1739, may be classified as a frontiersman, and only one came from the bottom rung of the social scale for colonial whites, that of indentured servitude. The occupations of several of the authors of briefer accounts are unknown.

The area and the Indian tribes visited by the travelers reveal much about the development of the Southern colonies between 1660 and 1763. In the half-century following the Restoration, many of the settlers of Virginia were interested in exploiting the land and resources of the Piedmont, and the proprietors of the Carolinas sought successful settlement of their vast domain. Consequently, most of the travelers of this period were explorers of the Piedmont and the Carolina coast or were early colonists of South Carolina. These individuals primarily encountered small tribes belonging to the Siouan language group, including the Saponi, Congaree, and Cape Fear Indians.

Toward the end of this period and continuing until 1763, there appeared accounts of remnants of Indian tribes that had been pacified by the English. After the Tuscarora War the natives along the South Atlantic coast were destroyed, driven west, or forced into dependent status, and travelers in the area were intrigued by these nations in decline.

In the fifty years before 1763, the Indians of major concern to the English in the Southeast were the Cherokees and Creeks. Each tribe was large, and each was important to the British government and its colonies in the struggle with France and Spain over control of the transmontane region. Perhaps indicative of the importance attached to the Cherokees and Creeks was the fact that nearly half of the accounts dating from this period dealt with these two tribes. During the same half century, a very small group of Indians, the Yamacraws, also received considerable attention. These Muskogean-speaking natives were helpful in the settlement of Georgia, but for reasons that are not readily apparent, more accounts exist of them than of any other identifiable group of Indians for the entire period under study. None of the records of the Yamacraws, however, was lengthy or detailed.

If the number of their comments and the length of their remarks may be taken as an indication of their interests, the British travelers were mainly concerned with the appearance of the South-eastern natives, their religious beliefs and practices, their villages and habitations, and their subsistence activities. The number and length of the comments were about equal for each of the elements within Indian society and culture, and approximately half of the European visitors recorded their observations on these traits of native civilization. Not all of these travelers commented on each trait, nor did they write with the same degree of intensity or insight, but considerably more attention was given to these elements of native life than to any other attributes of the red men. Slightly more than one-fourth of the travelers commented on the social customs of the Indians, while only slightly fewer referred to warfare. The strange and exciting dances of the natives, their medicine, and the reception given the whites were also frequently mentioned. Several of the visitors also revealed their over-all impression or reaction to the Indians. Sometimes the general impression was not openly stated, but the majority of the English seem to have had definite feelings about the native Americans.

Observations on the appearance of the Indian men and women and their dwellings were often the first comments made by the travelers. Skin color and the widespread practice of tattooing immediately attracted the visitors. The costume or its absence and the ornaments worn by both sexes also impressed the Europeans. The religious practices were naturally of special interest to ministers, but Englishmen of other professions and with other primary concerns also displayed curiosity toward native religion. Few of the travelers went as far as Robert Beverley, who plied an Indian with alcohol in order to obtain information, but nearly all of the more detailed accounts contained observations on this aspect of Indian culture. Most of them, however, revealed little understanding and even less sympathy for Indian religious beliefs. Perhaps because the homes and settlements of the natives were easily observed, records of their appearance were often made. Few details were normally given; usually the writer contented himself with the assertion that such houses looked like "loafs" or that villages were defended with palisades. The economic life of the Southern Indians, essentially the hunting activities of the men and the horticulture of the women, were also noted. Most of the visitors provided few or no descriptions of the methods of hunting and of food growing. A common conclusion drawn from the observation of Indian economic practices was that the men were lazy because they "only" hunted.

If the four items of major interest received superficial consideration, remarks regarding the less dramatic and more complex social customs such as marriage revealed an almost total lack of understanding. Aside from statements on the ease of divorce and condemnations or defenses of Indian maidens' moral standards, the travelers were usually silent on domestic customs or relationships within family, village, and tribe. Considering the danger posed to many of the English colonists by warring Indians, it is somewhat surprising that fewer than one-fourth of the whites even mentioned Indian warfare. The accounts used in this study were written by men who traveled in times of peace, and such persons evidently had little interest in the strange, cruel aspects of native fighting. There was little sympathy for the methods of warfare, but the remarks were neither as condemnatory or frightening, nor as numerous as might have been expected.

Comments on political organization were occasionally made. Probably because of their familiarity with a monarchical system of government, almost all of these travelers misunderstood native government and read into the Indians' governmental structure elements of monarchy. Small groups of Indians were usually considered to have been ruled by "kings," and large tribes such as the Creeks and the Cherokees were believed to have "emperors." Perhaps such designations became more appropriate by mid-eighteenth century, because the political organization of some Indians seems to have responded to European influence by acquiring some of the trappings of monarchy.[1]

The dances and the medical practices of the native American

---

[1] For a recent study of Cherokee political organization during the colonial period and the effect of European influences, see Frederick O. Gearing, *Priests and Warriors; Social Structures for Cherokee Politics in the Eighteenth Century.*

received some notice. More travelers commented upon the dances than on medicine, but the comments on the latter were usually more detailed. Few if any of the visitors attempted to understand the significance of the dances, and except for occasional praise for the effectiveness of some herb used by the Indians, native medical customs were also reported without comprehension of their importance.

Several travelers commented on the receptions given them and dealt with the broader aspects of white-Indian relations. Most of the visitors were welcomed by the natives. The friendliness usually continued throughout the sojourn, and it was reflected in the generally amiable impressions of the Englishmen. Very few of the whites voiced universal condemnation of the Indians. The strongest criticism usually came from ministers who were frustrated in their efforts to convert the Indians to Christianity. Ministers who had more limited contact retained their hope and belief in the friendliness of the native Americans. As with the number of comments on warfare, perhaps fewer of the visitors than might have been expected commented on white-Indian relations. Friendship with the Indians was important to the colonists, but only about one-fourth of the Englishmen made any comment concerning the need for peace. Most of these were vague expressions of the benefits to be gained from improved relations and condemnations of dishonesty in dealing with the Southeastern Indians. The practices of Indian traders were often condemned, but the travelers rarely had any constructive suggestions. Few of them advanced any comprehensive plan for relations between Indians and whites; a few considered that intermarriage might be the answer. Totally lacking on the part of the Europeans was any recognition of the profound nature of the conflict between the two civilizations.

Another aspect of white-Indian contact was the acceptance of certain European cultural items by the Southern Indians. The period was one of permissive, or non-directed, acculturation. The whites exercised little direct control over the Indians, and the items accepted by the natives were those that caused little disruption of native culture and society. European weapons, useful in both warfare and hunting, iron tools, and certain domesticated plants and animals were quickly accepted by the Indians; but attempts to introduce other elements of white civilization such as Christianity were frustrated. Acceptance of material items seems to be a fixed part of the initial pattern of acculturation of North American Indians by European civilization. But resistance to Christianity continued during the nineteenth century and was not confined to the Southeastern Indians. Few if any of the writers had insight into the acculturation process that was underway, but several commented on the acceptance of white cultural items.[2]

The travelers evidently were practical men, little given to abstract thought or philosophical speculation. For example, suggestions about the origins of the native Americans were rare. Unlike the controversy that developed between certain Spanish writers and their supporters in other European countries following the initial contact, the British visitors were not interested in the reasons for the Indians' presence in the New World.[3] Statements indicative of the author's racial beliefs were seldom made. Few of these men appeared to have any aversion to the Indian because of his race, but there was little open praise. During the colonial period, the British generally believed that the Negro was inferior, but the travelers' racial attitudes are not that apparent. Some of the writers criticized the Indian male as being "lazy"; however, none of these men connected the supposed vice with racial origins.

The men also revealed little interest either in contributing to or detracting from the concept of the "Noble Savage." The eighteenth-century *philosophes* may have been influenced by some of the writings, and some twentieth-century scholars believe that a particular account "epitomized" the "Noble Savage" concept or that the better-known travelers drew numerous parallels between the Indians and the ancient Greeks and Romans.[4] But for the large majority of the so-

---

[2] Berkhofer, *Salvation and the Savage*; and Edward H. Spicer *et al.*, *Perspectives in American Indian Culture Change*, 539.

[3] On the controversy, see Huddleston, *Origin of the American Indian*.

[4] For example, see Diket, "Noble Savage Epitomized in 'A New Voyage to Carolina,'" and Pearce, *Savages of America*, chap. i.

journers the Indians were too real to be idealized, and the comments linking the natives and the ancients were insignificant when compared to the total number of observations.

Despite the restricted interests of the white visitors, their writings provide much of the present-day knowledge of the Southern tribes. The colonial data have been supplemented by other sources, but the studies of anthropologists such as John R. Swanton and historians such as David H. Corkran reveal the magnitude of the colonial contributions.

The study of British travelers among the Southern Indians during the century following 1660 not only reveals the nature of the whites' interest in the native Americans, but also provides some insight into the culture of the travelers themselves. Examination of the reasons for traveling, the nature of the comments, and the omission of observations concerning certain aspects of native civilization indicate that, on the whole, the British were a practical people. Few if any of the men deliberately visited the Indians unless they were on official business; probably indicative of the reluctance to undertake the hardships and dangers of wilderness travel solely for pleasure was the fact that no account by a woman was discovered. Once the Indians were encountered, the Europeans centered their observations on the material items of native culture and revealed little interest in nonmaterial aspects of Indian civilization. Some of the observations dealt with the strange, curious appearance of the natives and their way of life, but many were of a practical nature. The British colonists were primarily interested in the maintenance of peaceful relations with the Indians, in increasing the influence of the British, and in materially or spiritually profiting from their contact, and the white travelers were concerned with recording knowledge that might further these goals.

Bibliography

Primary Sources, Manuscript and Printed

Alsop, George. *Character of the Province of Maryland.* London, 1666.

Alvord, Clarence W., and Lee Bidgood, ed. *First Explorations of the Trans-Allegheny Region by the Virginians, 1650–1674.* Cleveland, 1912.

Archdale, John. *New Description of that Fertile and Pleasant Province of Carolina.* London, 1707.

[Ashe, Thomas.]. *Carolina; or a Description of the Present State of that Country, and the Natural Excellencies Thereof.* London, 1682.

Beverley, Robert. *History and Present State of Virginia.* Ed. Louis B. Wright. Chapel Hill, 1947.

Bownas, Samuel. *Account of the Life, Travels, and Christian Experiences in the Work of the Ministry of Samuel Bownas.* Ed. J. Besse. London, 1756.

Burnaby, Andrew. *Travels through the Middle Settlements in North America.* Repr. ed. of 2nd ed. Ithaca, 1960.

Byrd, William [II]. *Another Secret Diary of William Byrd of Westover, 1739–1741.* Ed. Maude H. Woodfin and Marion Tinling. Richmond, 1942.

———. *Histories of the Dividing Line Betwixt Virginia and North Carolina.* Ed. William K. Boyd. Raleigh, 1929.

———. *London Diary (1717–1721) and Other Writings.* Ed. Louis B. Wright and Marion Tinling. New York, 1958.

———. *Prose Works, Narratives of a Colonial Virginian.* Ed. Louis B. Wright. Cambridge, 1966.

————. *Secret Diary of William Byrd of Westover, 1709–1712.* Ed. Louis B. Wright and Marion Tinling. Richmond, 1941.

Candler, Allen D., ed. *Colonial Records of Georgia, 1738–1744.* 26 vols. Atlanta, 1904–16.

Carroll, Bartholomew R., ed. *Historical Collections of South Carolina; . . . from Its First Discovery to . . . 1776.* 2 vols. New York, 1836.

Catesby, Mark. *Natural History of Carolina, Florida, and the Bahama Islands.* 2 vols. London, 1731–43.

Chalkley, Thomas. *Journal or Historical Account of the Life, Travels, and Christian Experiences of . . . Thomas Chalkley.* 2nd ed. New York, 1808.

Courtenay, William A., ed. *Genesis of South Carolina, 1562–1670.* Columbia, 1907.

Cumming, William P., ed. *Southeast in Early Maps.* 2nd ed. Chapel Hill, 1962.

Dunlop, Captain. "Capt. Dunlop's Voyage to the Southward, 1687," *South Carolina Historical and Genealogical Magazine*, Vol. XXX (July, 1929), 127–33.

Edmundson, William. *Journal of the Life, Travels, Sufferings, and Labour of Love in the Work of . . . William Edmundson.* London, 1713.

Egmont, John Percival, First Earl of, *Diary of Viscount Percival, Afterwards First Earl of Egmont.* Ed. Historical Manuscripts Commission. 3 vols. London, 1920–23.

————. *Journal of the Earl of Egmont: Abstract of the Trustees' Proceedings for Establishing the Colony of Georgia, 1732–1738.* Ed. Robert G. McPherson. Wormsloe Found. *Publications*, No. 5; Athens, 1962.

[Farmer, John.] "First American Journey, 1711–1714." Ed. H. J. Cadbury. American Antiquarian Soc. *Proceedings*, n. s., Vol. LIII; Worcester, 1944.

Fontaine, Jacques. *Memoirs of a Huguenot Family.* Ed. and trans. Ann Maury. Repr. ed. New York, 1907.

Fox, George. *Journal or Historical Account of the Life, Travels, Suffering, Christian Experiences and Labour of Love of . . . George Fox.* Ed. Rufus M. Jones. New York, 1963.

Fyffe, William. "Letter to Brother John, February 1, 1761." Thomas

Gilcrease Institute of American History and Art, Manuscript Division. Tulsa, Okla.

Georgia Historical Society. *Collections.* 4 vols. in 5. Savannah, 1840–42; New York, 1848–73.

Gibbon, John. *Introductio ad Blasoniam, or an Essay to a More Correct Blazon in Latine than Hath Formerly Been Used.* London, 1682.

Glover, Thomas. *Account of Virginia.* Oxford, 1904.

Gordon, Peter. *Journal of Peter Gordon, 1732–1735.* Ed. E. Merton Coulter. Wormsloe Found. *Publications,* No. 6. Athens, 1963.

Grant, Ludovick. "Historical Relation of Facts Delivered by Ludovick Grant, Indian Trader, to His Excellency the Governor of South Carolina," *South Carolina Historical and Genealogical Magazine,* Vol. X (Jan., 1909), 54–68.

Griffith, John. *Journal of the Life, Travels, and Labours in the Work of the Ministry of John Griffith.* London, 1779.

Hall, Clayton C., ed. *Narratives of Early Maryland, 1633–1684.* Repr. ed. New York, 1958.

[Hall, F.] *Importance of the British Plantations in America to This Kingdom.* London, 1731.

Herbert, John. *Journal of Colonel John Herbert, Commissioner of Indian Affairs for the Province of South Carolina.* Ed. Alexander S. Salley. Columbia, 1936.

Hewat, Alexander. *Historical Account of the Rise and Progress of the Colonies of South Carolina and Georgia.* 2 vols. London, 1779.

Hilton, William. "The Relacon of the Late Discovery Made in Florida." Royal Society Classified Papers. Vol. VII, Pt. 1. Photostatic copy. Library of Congress, Manuscript Division.

Holme, Benjamin. *Collections of the Epistles and Works.* London, 1754.

Humphreys, David. *Historical Account of the Incorporated Society for the Propagation of the Gospel in Foreign Parts . . . to the Year 1728.* 2 vols. London, 1730.

Hunter, George. *George Hunter's Map of the Cherokee Country and the Path Thereto in 1730.* Ed. Alexander S. Salley. Hist. Comm. of S. C., *Bulletin* 4; Columbia, 1917.

Jones, Hugh. *Present State of Virginia.* Repr. ed. New York, 1865.

Lawson, John. *New Voyage to Carolina.* London, 1709.

————. *New Voyage to Carolina.* Ed. Hugh T. Lefler. Chapel Hill, 1967.

Lederer, John. *Discoveries of John Lederer, with Unpublished Letters by and about Lederer to Governor John Winthrop, Jr.* Ed. William P. Cumming. Charlottesville, 1958.

Le Jau, Francis. *Carolina Chronicle of Dr. Francis Le Jau, 1706–1717.* Ed. Frank J. Klingberg. Univ. of Calif. *Publications in History,* Vol. LIII. Berkeley, 1956.

McDowell, William L., Jr., ed. *Documents Relating to Indian Affairs, May 21, 1750–August 7, 1754.* Columbia, 1958.

————, ed. *Documents Relating to Indian Affairs, 1754–1765.* Columbia, 1962.

————, ed. *Journals of the Commissioners of the Indian Trade, September 20, 1710–August 29, 1718.* Columbia, 1955.

Mereness, Newton D., ed. *Travels in the American Colonies, 1690–1783.* Repr. ed. New York, 1961.

Moore, Francis. *Voyage to Georgia, Begun in the Year 1735.* London, 1744.

"Narrative of a Voyage to Maryland, 1705–1706," *American Historical Review,* Vol. XII (Jan., 1907), 327–40.

New Voyage to Georgia, by a Young Gentleman. London, 1735.

Oglethorpe, James E. *Account of the Colony of Georgia.* London, 1732.

————. *Letters from General Oglethorpe.* Ga. Hist. Soc., *Collections,* Vol. III. New York, 1848.

————. *New and Accurate Account of the Province of Georgia.* London, 1732.

Peckham, Howard H., ed. *Captured by Indians; True Tales of Pioneer Survivors.* New Brunswick, 1954.

"R. F." "The Present State of Carolina with Advice to the Settlers, by R.F." Transcript copy. Library of Congress, Manuscript Division.

Richardson, William. "An Account of my Proceedings since I Accepted the Indian Mission in October 2d, 1758." New York Public Library, Wilberforce Eames Collection, Manuscript Division.

Salley, Alexander S., ed. *Journal of the Commissioners of the Indian Trade of South Carolina, September 20, 1710–April 12, 1715.* Columbia, 1926.

————, ed. *Narratives of Early Carolina, 1650–1708.* Repr. ed. New York, 1958.

Saunders, William L., ed. *Colonial Records of North Carolina.* 10 vols. Raleigh, 1886–90.

Society for the Propagation of the Gospel in Foreign Parts. "Journals of Proceedings of the Society." 57 vols. Photostatic copy. Library of Congress, Manuscript Division.

————. "Letters and Reports of the Missionaries, Eighteenth Century." Series A (Contemporary copies), 26 vols.; Series B (Original letters), 25 vols. Transcript copy. Library of Congress, Manuscript Division.

Spotswood, Alexander. *Official Letters of Alexander Spotswood, Lieutenant-Governor of the Colony of Virginia, 1710–1722.* Ed. R. A. Brock. 2 vols. Richmond, 1882.

Story, Thomas. *Journal of the Life of Thomas Story.* Newcastle-on-Tyne, 1747.

Thickness, Philip. *Memoirs and Anecdotes of Philip Thickness, late Lieutenant Governor of Land Guard Fort, and unfortunately Father of George Touchet, Baron Audley.* 3 vols. London, 1788–91.

Timberlake, Henry. *Memoirs of Lieut. Henry Timberlake.* London, 1765.

————. *Lieut. Henry Timberlake's Memoirs.* Ed. Samuel C. Williams. Repr. ed. Marietta, 1948.

"Tour into the Indian Nations, 1740–42." Stowe Manuscripts, No. 792. British Museum. Transcript copy. Library of Congress, Manuscript Division.

Washburn, Wilcomb E., ed. *Indian and the White Man.* Garden City, 1964.

Washington, George. *Diaries of George Washington, 1748–1799.* Ed. John C. Fitzpatrick. 4 vols. Boston, 1925.

Wesley, Charles. *Journal of the Rev. Charles Wesley: The Early Journal, 1736–1739.* Ed. John Telford. London, 1909.

Wesley, John. *Journal of the Rev. John Wesley, A.M.* Ed. Nehemiah Curnock. 8 vols. London [1909–16].

————. *Letters of the Rev. John Wesley, A. M.* Ed. John Telford. 8 vols. London [1931].

Williams, Samuel C., ed. *Early Travels in the Tennessee Country, 1540–1800*. Johnson City, 1928.

Woodmason, Charles. *Carolina Backcountry on the Eve of the Revolution*. Ed. Richard J. Hooker. Chapel Hill, 1953.

Books and Articles

Abernethy, Thomas P. *Three Virginia Frontiers*. Baton Rouge, 1940.

———. *Western Lands and the American Revolution*. New York, 1937.

Adams, Percy G. *Travelers and Travel Liars, 1660–1800*. Berkeley, 1962.

Alden, John R. *John Stuart and the Southern Colonial Frontier, 1754–1775*. Univ. of Mich. *Publications in Hist. and Pol. Sci.*, Vol. XV; Ann Arbor, 1944.

Alvord, Clarence W. *Mississippi Valley in British Politics*. Cleveland, 1917.

Barnwell, J. W. "Dr. Henry Woodward, the First English Settler in South Carolina, and Some of His Descendants," *South Carolina Historical and Genealogical Magazine*, Vol. VII (Jan., 1907), 29–41.

Berkhofer, Robert F., Jr. *Salvation and the Savage: An Analysis of Protestant Missions and the American Indian Response, 1787–1862*. [Lexington], 1965.

Billington, Ray A. *Westward Expansion: A History of the American Frontier*. 2nd ed. New York, 1960.

Bissell, Benjamin H. *American Indian in English Literature of the Eighteenth Century*. Yale Univ. *Studies in English*, Vol. LXVIII. New Haven, 1925.

Bloom, Leonard. "The Acculturation of the Eastern Cherokee: Historical Aspects," *North Carolina Historical Review*, Vol. XIX (Oct., 1942), 323–58.

Bourne, Edward G. "The Travels of Jonathan Carver," *American Historical Review*, Vol. XI (Jan., 1906), 287–302.

Brebner, John B. *Explorers of North America, 1492–1806*. New York, 1933.

Brown, Douglas Summers. *Catawba Indians: The People of the River*. Columbia, 1966.

Bushnell, David I., Jr. *Native Villages and Village Sites East of the*

Mississippi. Bureau of American Ethnology *Bulletin 69.* Washington, 1919.

Cannon, William B. "John Wesley's Years in Georgia," *Methodist History*, Vol. I (July, 1963), 1–7.

Carpenter, Delma R. "The Route Followed by Governor Spotswood in 1716 across the Blue Ridge Mountains," *Virginia Magazine of History and Biography*, Vol. LXXIII (Oct., 1965), 405–12.

Clark, Thomas D., ed. *Travels in the Old South: A Bibliography.* 3 vols. Norman, 1948–56.

Corkran, David H. *Cherokee Frontier, Conflict and Survival, 1740–62.* Norman, 1962.

———. *Creek Frontier, 1540–1783.* Norman, 1967.

———. "The Sacred Fires of the Cherokees," *Southern Indian Studies,* Vol. V (Oct., 1953), 21–26.

Coulter, E. Merton. "Mary Musgrove, 'Queen of the Creeks': A Chapter of Early Georgia Troubles," *Georgia Historical Quarterly*, Vol. XI (Mar., 1927), 1–30.

———. "When John Wesley Preached in Georgia," *Georgia Historical Quarterly*, Vol. IX (Dec., 1925), 317–51.

Crane, Verner W. *The Southern Frontier, 1670–1732.* Durham, 1928.

———. "The Tennessee River as the Road to Carolina: the Beginnings of Exploration and Trade," *Mississippi Valley Historical Review*, Vol. III (June, 1916), 3–18.

Cumming, William P. "Geographical Misconceptions of the Southeast in the Cartography of the Seventeenth and Eighteenth Centuries," *Journal of Southern History*, Vol. IV (Nov., 1938), 476–93.

Diket, A. L. "The Noble Savage Convention as Epitomized in John Lawson's 'A New Voyage to Carolina,'" *North Carolina Historical Review*, Vol. XLIII (Oct., 1966), 413–29.

Dodson, Leonidas. *Alexander Spotswood, Governor of Colonial Virginia, 1710–1732.* Philadelphia, 1932.

Dozier, Edward P. "Forced and Permissive Acculturation," *American Indian*, Vol. VII (Spring, 1955), 38–44.

Drake, Samuel G. "Early History of Georgia and Sir Alexander Cuming's Embassy to the Cherokee," *New England Historical and Genealogical Register*, Vol. XXVI (July, 1872), 260–71.

Driver, Harold E. *Indians of North America*. Chicago, 1961.

———, et al. *Indian Tribes of North America*. Indiana Univ. Publ. in Anthro. and Linguistics, *Memoir*, No. 9. Baltimore, 1953.

Dunbar, Seymour. *History of Travel in America*. 4 vols. Repr. ed. New York, 1937.

Fairchild, Hoxie N. *Noble Savage: A Study in Romantic Naturalism*. New York, 1928.

Fenton, William N. *American Indian and White Relations to 1830*. Chapel Hill, 1957.

Franklin, W. Neil. "Virginia and the Cherokee Indian Trade, 1753–1775," East Tenn. Hist. Soc. *Publications*, Vol. V (Jan., 1933), 22–38.

———. "Virginia and the Cherokee Indian Trade, 1673–1752," East Tenn. Hist. Soc. *Publications*, Vol. IV (Jan., 1932), 3–21.

Freeman, Douglas S. *George Washington, a Biography*. 6 vols. New York, 1948–54.

Fundaburk, Emma L. *Southeastern Indians, Life Portraits; A Catalogue of Pictures, 1564–1860*. Luverne, 1958.

———, and Mary D. F. Foreman. *Sun Circles and Human Hands: The Southeastern Indians—Art and Industry*. Luverne, 1957.

Gearing, Frederick O. *Priests and Warriors; Social Structures for Cherokee Politics in the Eighteenth Century*. American Anthro. Assoc. *Memoir* 93. [Menasha, 1962].

Gilbert, William H. "Eastern Cherokees," Bureau of American Ethnology *Bulletin 133*. Washington, 1943, 169–413.

Greene, Evarts B. "The Anglican Outlook on the American Colonies in the Early Eighteenth Century," *American Historical Review*, Vol. XX (Oct., 1914), 64–85.

Harris, Walter A. *Here the Creeks Sat Down*. Marion, 1958.

Hiden, Martha W., and Henry M. Dargan. "John Gibbon's Manuscript Notes Concerning Virginia," *Virginia Magazine of History and Biography*, Vol. LXXIV (Jan., 1966), 3–22.

Hodge, Frederick W., ed. *Handbook of American Indians, North of Mexico*. 2 vols. Bureau of American Ethnology *Bulletin 30*. Washington, 1907–10.

Huddleston, Lee E. *Origins of the American Indians: European Concepts, 1492–1729*. Austin, 1967.

Hyde, George E. *Indians of the Woodlands: From Prehistoric Times to 1725.* Norman, 1962.

Jones, Charles C., Jr. *Historical Sketch of Tomo-chi-chi, Mico of the Yamacraws.* Albany, 1868.

Jordan, Winthrop D. *White over Black: The Development of American Attitudes toward the Negro, 1550–1812.* Chapel Hill, 1968.

Juricek, John T. "The Westo Indians," *Ethnohistory*, Vol. XI (Spring, 1964), 134–73.

Keiser, Albert. *Indian in American Literature.* New York, 1933.

Kirkham, E. Bruce. "The First English Editions of John Lawson's 'Voyage to Carolina': A Bibliographical Study," *Bibliographical Society of America Papers*, Vol. LXI (1967), 258–65.

Klingberg, Frank L. "The Indian Frontier in South Carolina as Seen by the S.P.G. Missionary," *Journal of Southern History*, Vol. V (Nov., 1939), 478–500.

McCrady, Edward. *History of South Carolina under the Proprietary Government, 1670–1719.* New York, 1897.

———. *History of South Carolina under the Royal Government, 1719–1776.* New York, 1899.

Meriwether, Robert L. *Expansion of South Carolina, 1729–1765.* Kingsport, 1940.

Mook, Maurice A. "The Anthropological Position of the Indian Tribes of Tidewater Virginia," *William and Mary College Quarterly Historical Magazine*, 2nd ser., Vol. XXIII (Jan., 1943), 27–40.

Mooney, James. "Myths of the Cherokees," Bureau of American Ethnology *Nineteenth Annual Report*, 3–548. Washington, 1897–98.

———. "The Sacred Formulas of the Cherokees," Bureau of American Ethnology *Seventh Annual Report*, 301–97. Washington, 1891.

Morton, Richard L. *Colonial Virginia.* 2 vols. Chapel Hill, 1960.

———. "The Reverend Hugh Jones, Lord Baltimore's Mathematician," *William and Mary Quarterly*, 3rd ser., Vol. VII (Jan., 1950), 107–15.

Murdock, George P. *Ethnographic Bibliography of North America.* 2nd ed. New Haven, 1953.

Myer, William E. "Indian Trails of the Southeast," Bureau of American Ethnology *Forty-second Annual Report*, 727–857. Washington, 1928.

Pascoe, Charles F. *Two Hundred Years of the S. P. G.: An Historical*

Account of the Society for the Propagation of the Gospel in Foreign Parts, 1701–1900. London, 1901.

Pearce, Roy H. *Savages of America, a Study of the Indian and the Idea of Civilization.* Rev. ed. Baltimore, 1965.

Rand, James H. *North Carolina Indians.* James Sprunt Hist. *Publications,* Vol. XII, No. 2. Chapel Hill, 1913.

Reese, Trevor R. "A Red Indian Visit to Eighteenth-Century England," *History Today,* Vol. IV (May, 1954), 334–37.

Rightmyer, Nelson. "Hugh Jones, Colonial Enigma," *Maryland Historical Magazine,* Vol. XLVII (Sept., 1952), 263–64.

Rights, Douglas L. *American Indian in North Carolina.* 2nd ed. Winston-Salem, 1957.

―――. "The Trading Path to the Indians," *North Carolina Historical Review,* Vol. VIII (Oct., 1931), 403–26.

Robinson, W. Stitt, Jr. "Indian Education and Missions in Colonial Virginia," *Journal of Southern History,* Vol. XVIII (May, 1952), 152–68.

Rothrock, Mary U. "Carolina Traders among the Overhill Cherokees, 1690–1760," East Tenn. Hist. Soc. *Publications,* Vol. I (Jan., 1929), 3–18.

Rutman, Darrett B., ed. *Old Dominion: Essays for Thomas Perkins Abernethy.* Charlottesville, 1964.

Saum, Lewis O. *Fur Trader and the Indian.* Seattle, 1965.

Schmidt, Martin. *Young Wesley: Missionary and Theologian of Missions.* Trans. L. A. Fletcher. London, 1958.

Simon, John S. *John Wesley and the Religious Societies.* London, 1921.

Smith, James M., ed. *Seventeenth-Century America: Essays in Colonial History.* Chapel Hill, 1959.

Social Science Research Council Summer Seminar on Acculturation, 1953. "Acculturation: An Explanatory Formulation," *American Anthropologist,* n. s., Vol. LVI (Dec., 1954), 973–1002.

Speck, Frank G. "The Question of Matrilineal Descent in the Southeastern Siouan Area," *American Anthropologist,* n. s., Vol. XL (Jan., 1938), 1–12.

Spencer, Robert F., *et al. Native Americans.* New York, 1965.

Spicer, Edward H., *et al.*, ed. *Perspectives in American Indian Culture Change.* Chicago, 1961.

Stuart, Meriwether. "Textual Notes on 'John Gibbon's Manuscript Notes Concerning Virginia,' " *Virginia Magazine of History and Biography*, Vol. LXXIV (Oct., 1966), 462–79.

Swanton, John R. *Indians of the Southeastern United States*. 2 vols. Bureau of American Ethnology *Bulletin 137*. Washington, 1946.

———. *Early History of the Creek Indians and Their Neighbors*. Bureau of American Ethnology *Bulletin 73*. Washington, 1922.

———. *Myths and Tales of the Southeastern Indians*. Bureau of American Ethnology *Bulletin 88*. Washington, 1929.

———. "Religious Beliefs and Medical Practices of the Indians of the Creek Confederacy," Bureau of American Ethnology *Forty-second Annual Report*, 477–636. Washington, 1928.

———. "Social Organization and Social Usages of the Indians of the Creek Confederation," Bureau of American Ethnology *Forty-second Annual Report*, 23–672. Washington, 1928.

Tyerman, Luke. *Oxford Methodists: Memoirs of the Rev. Messrs. Clayton, Ingham, Gambold, Hervey, and Broughton*. New York, 1873.

Tyler, Moses C. *History of American Literature, 1607–1765*. Repr. ed. Ithaca, 1949.

Williams, Samuel C. "An Account of the Presbyterian Mission to the Cherokees, 1751–1759," *Tennessee Historical Magazine*, 2nd ser., Vol. I (Jan., 1931), 125–38.

Willis, William S. "Patrilineal Institutions in Southeastern North America," *Ethnohistory*, Vol. X (Summer, 1963), 250–69.

Wissler, Clark. *American Indian, an Introduction to the Anthropology of the New World*. Repr. ed. of 3rd ed. New York, 1950.

Wright, Louis B. *First Gentlemen of Virginia: Intellectual Qualities of the Early Colonial Ruling Class*. Charlottesville, 1964.

129885

E   Randolph, J. Ralph,
78   1935-.
S6.5
R3   British travelers
          among the southern
          Indians, 1660-1763

DATE		
MAR 27 1995		